Magnetic Core Memory Decoded
Developing a Magnetic Core Memory System

A practical approach to designing and building a working Magnetic Core Memory system from theory to a working prototype.

Edition 1

J. S. Walker

First published in the United Kingdom in 2021 by

Oldfangled Publishing

ISBN 978-0-9957072-1-4

Contents

Chapter 1   - Introduction...7
    Magnetic Core Logic...23
Chapter 2   – Principles of operation 25
    Ferrite Properties...25
    Square-Loop Ferrite 28
    Read Operation Current Polarities 40
    Write Operation Current Polarities 41
Chapter 3   – Selecting a Suitable Ferrite Core 43
    Testing cores and characterising for design.................................43
    Sense Output Detection...59
    Coincidence Principle...63
    Inhibit Action...64
    Memory Write 65
    Memory Read 66
    Selection Wire Drivers...67
    Sense Amplifier and Inhibit Drivers 67
    Control Logic 67
Chapter 4   – Designing the Core Array 69
    64 byte (8x8x8) 69
Chapter 5   – Designing the address decoder.................................83
    Write Mode Phase 92
    Read Mode Phase 93
    Control Logic Features 95
Chapter 6   – Memory Cycle Trigger.................................97
Chapter 7   – Read Sense Amplifier 103
Chapter 8   – Current Source Pulse Generator.................................121
Chapter 9   – Inhibit Driver...139
    Inhibit Wire Function 141
Chapter 10   – Control Logic 151
    Idle Mode 152
    Write Mode Sequence...153
    Read Mode Sequence...154
    Read Cycle Logic...157
    Write Mode Logic...173
    Memory Speed...177
Chapter 11   - Testing the Memory...179
    Transconductance 188
Chapter 12   - Further Development...193
Chapter 13   - Assembling a Core Array 197
    Fitting the X Selection Wires 201
    Fitting the Y Selection Wires 202
Chapter 14   - Rope Memory 205

How is Data Read from Rope Memory 206
Inhibit Wires in a Rope Memory... 210
Appendix A – Magnetic Core Memory Summary... 215
List of Figures 217

Magnetic Core Memory Decoded

ℒ ℋℰ

Chapter 1 - Introduction

Computers have been around in one form or another for hundreds or even thousands of years depending on what you believe qualifies a machine to be classified as a computer.

For the purpose of explanation in this book I will use the term 'computer' to describe a machine which has been designed for use in processing data in a specific way and outputs information which varies depending on the input data.

Early computers which are included in this category are machines such as the abacus an example of which is shown in figure 1-1.

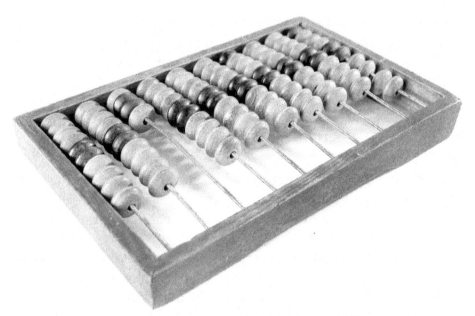

Figure 1-1 An Abacus - some dating back over 4000 years

The abacus was used to calculate mathematical products based on the values initially set on its number indication beads.

It was not automated but when used in the proper way it was a reliable way to perform mathematical calculations. The input values in these calculations were entered into a set of beads by placing them in specific positions.

These beads could be considered to be a data storage mechanism or 'register' as it would be referred to in more recent terminology.

The result it produced was indicated in another set of beads and again this can be considered a data register.

Without the ability to represent data in a meaningful way the abacus would be of no practical use and although its bead indication system was not really considered to be data registers it could easily be argued that that if such a device was to be emulated in a more modern system then the data storage elements would be referred to as 'registers'.

As mathematics and engineering technology developed the amount of mathematical work being carried out in order to support it began to grow rapidly and to such an extent that dedicated calculators were created.

Initially a calculator was not a mechanical or electrical machine but a person who was employed to perform mathematical functions although the methods they used to carry out the actual mathematics varied a great deal.

The role of calculators grew in scope and importance as the world developed and in particular the increasing application of financial and engineering systems required a great deal of accurate and often complex mathematics.

As ever, wars also played a major role in development as tables needed to be calculated for a variety of reasons and at the same time the need for accurate navigation further added to the need for increasingly complex mathematics.

An inevitable consequence of this requirement was the desire by many engineers and mathematicians to create machines which were capable of producing results more quickly and with fewer errors than was possible using human calculators.

And so the emergence of simple mechanical calculators began and over time these mechanical calculators increased in complexity and performance.

One aspect that was almost universal in their conceptual operation and design was the need to enter at least two data values into them on which the calculator could then perform some predefined mathematical operation.

As with the abacus the data input mechanisms could be considered to be data storage registers and as these calculators continued to develop they often included additional registers to hold further intermediate and output data values.

Figure 1-2 shows an example of an early mechanical calculator dating back to the very early 1900's.

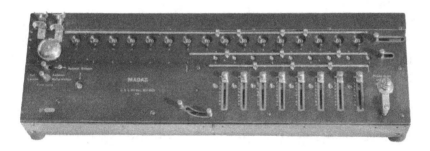

Figure 1-2 Early mechanical calculator

It can be seen in figure 1-2 that the calculator can accept and store or retain data values entered into it by the operator and it can also store data values in its output indicator register.

In both the abacus and the mechanical calculator the data values entered by the operator are retained and so the mechanism in which they are stored can be considered to be memory.

It is no coincidence that as computers developed the designers included in them some means by which to store data values and in fact these data storage registers are the key to the operation of all computers and the basic concepts and design have their roots in their mechanical ancestors.

Without some means to retain data in specific places which can be accessed by the computer then it would not be possible for a computer processor to perform any useful function.

Mechanical calculators are for the most part very limited in the way they can operate because they have fixed mechanisms and only very limited amounts of data can be stored in them at any one time.

If we consider applying the same limitations to a modern processor then no matter how powerful that processor may be if it could only access 2 or 3 fixed data value locations then it would not be any more useful than an abacus, although it would of course be somewhat faster.

As computer technology developed into the electronic realm, and also a few limited experiments with mechanical versions, then the requirement for the machine to store more data was always a limiting factor in how flexible they could be.

Adding more data storage, or memory, to a computer system is very easy today but during initial development of electronic computer systems in the 1940's though to the 1970's this was certainly not the case.

A huge amount of time and development effort was put into creating new technologies which could be used to deliver larger amounts of memory at a commercially acceptable cost.

One of the most important of these technologies was magnetic core memory and it is this technology that I shall be discussing throughout the remainder of this book.

As we delve into this technology it will rapidly become clear that the development of this memory technology was not only very ingenious but also far more complex than may first be assumed. Indeed it seemed to be so difficult and complex to develop that it can be hard to appreciate why such a lot of effort was expended on it at all. However it is important to remember that at the time this memory system was developed there were no serious alternatives which could be used to provide such large amounts of memory.

Early electronic memory consisted of either electro-mechanical relay type data storage or vacuum tube valve storage or other large and cumbersome methods of storing data as individual bits.

The need for larger memory storage capacity is obvious when you look at the number of different technologies which were developed in an attempt to meet the growing demands of computer development. Early designs ranged from revolving mechanical cylinders filled with hundreds of capacitors to banks of mechanical relays or acoustic delay lines.

It is very difficult today to appreciate why so many different approaches where attempted in order to find a solution to the data storage problem.

We are surrounded by an almost endless variety of cheap and effective electronic memory devices but back at the start of computer technology this was not the case.

It is also worth remembering that many of the engineers at that time were mechanical or electrical engineers and that can clearly be seen by the nature of some solutions which were attempted.

Some very ingenious ideas emerged and although most never made it into widespread use they are still marvels of engineering and inventiveness.

An example of this is the torsion wire delay line memory which used a stiff coil of wire and sent data in the form of torsion shock waves down this wire. The data was effectively stored as a pulse as it travelled down the wire and could be retrieved at the other end of the wire and repeated to keep the data 'stored' in the wire.

Although this type of device is very interesting it was not really practical for large scale memory systems and also was not able to retain data in the even of power failure.

Another example of early data storage was the rotating capacitor drum memory system in which a large number of capacitors were arranged inside a large drum assembly. The capacitors were wired to contacts on the surface of the drum and the drum rotated at relatively high speed. Data was stored in the capacitors in much the same way it is stored in a modern DRAM and was accessed through contacts as the drum rotated.

Many other solutions were tried with varying degrees of success but none of them were really practical for scaling up into much larger systems.

The problem with all early data storage designs was the enormous cost and huge physical space that each occupied. Power consumption was also a major consideration as the requirement for the amount of data storage quickly grew.

While implementing a few bytes was not difficult it rapidly became clear that at the time all currently existing data storage methods would never be suitable for implementing significant amounts of storage at a cost that would make it practical or commercially viable.

For example to store a single data bit using valve technology required at least one valve and so creating a memory system capable of storing 10k bytes would require 80,000 valves and this would result in a construction that would have been impractical in terms of cost, physical size and power consumption.

This type of memory was however fairly common and is really the basis for the design of SRAM devices although it was not a practical solution until the later development of large scale integrated circuits.

The problems of scalability were easily overcome by the advent of integrated circuit fabrication but this was not available in the 1950's.

One of the early magnetic memory cores which was implemented provided 256k bytes of memory space and while this is tiny today it was considered astronomical at the time. It is also true that the cost was enormous and this modest 256k bytes of memory cost almost $400,000.00 back in the 1960's which is equivalent to approximately $3.5 million at the time of writing.

In fact it is only a few years ago from the time of writing this that computer memory was still so expensive that it was not uncommon for business premises to be raided at night and the computers stripped of their memory modules. Such was the high value of these modules that an entire criminal black market emerged to handle and sell on these high value items.

Luckily as the cost of memory rapidly decreased then so did the black market trade and memory became cheap enough to render stealing it a fairly pointless exercise.

During early development most commercial computers had very modest amounts of memory but even so the cost was extremely high and often represented a significant percentage of the total value.

Initially the cost of core memory was approximately $1.00 per bit but as it was further developed and manufacturing was improved the cost dropped by over 100 times to less than $0.01 per bit.

This may sound cheap but consider that a modern micro SD card which is smaller than a postage stamp can hold 128Gb of data and so an equivalent core memory system would cost over $1 Billion. Fortunately modern microchip based memory can be manufactured millions of times more cheaply than core memory ever could be and as we proceed through the development of our own core memory system the reasons for this will become clear.

It was however clear that when magnetic core technology was first proposed back in the 1950's it would be able to offer a significant saving in production costs compared to the alternatives.

It also offered significant reductions in the physical size and power consumption of practical memory systems and this benefit would increase as the scale of memory systems grew.

During the 1960's magnetic core memory became the primary data storage technology used in computer systems and in other systems which needed to have electronic data storage.

This technology rapidly replaced existing memory systems and as it was developed and improved it allowed memory systems to be implemented on a scale that would have been unimaginable just a few years earlier.

Another advantage of magnetic core memory is that it is non volatile and was able to retain the stored data even if power was removed from the system. This was a feature which greatly added to the robustness of computer systems as it allowed data to be protected despite unreliable power supplies.

An offshoot to the random access memory systems which could be implemented using magnetic core technology was the so called 'rope memory' which could provide large amounts of read only memory or ROM and which was used to store information in a permanent form such as system program data or operating systems. This type of memory was extremely reliable once built and for that reason was used in systems such as the guidance computers in the Apollo space vehicles.

I will briefly describe the operation of read only magnetic core rope memory technology in a later chapter.

At this point I wish to make it clear that while there is a great deal of mathematical theory and design technology required in implementing a magnetic core system I will try to avoid this as much as possible throughout this book and will attempt to stick to practical methods for implementing our memory system.

A small amount of mathematical theory is unavoidable but I will keep this to a minimum and replace as much of it as possible with empirical tests and experimentation.

If you intend to build your own memory system then I would still highly recommend carrying out similar tests rather than jumping directly to assembling a finished system. Not only is this highly educational in terms of learning about the inner workings of magnetic core memory but it is also a lot of fun with some very interesting results.

I do not intend this book to be just a clinical explanation on the theory of magnetic memory technology but will be more of a practical, hands on, approach to developing a memory system.

This system will include the main features required to create a large scale magnetic core memory storage solution.

Large scale is of course a relative term and creating a magnetic core memory system that would compete with modern electronic data storage systems will of course not be feasible.

I do however hope that the information presented in this book will be of interest to anyone who is fascinated by the historical development of computer systems.

The story of magnetic core memory is long and very interesting from its inception in the 1940's it remained in widespread use until well into the 1970's and beyond.

It is now only really used in historical equipment but it is no less astounding how rapidly this technology advanced and how it helped to propel the design of ever more powerful computing machines which it did very successfully for over 30 years.

The early core memory development consisted of just a few large magnetic cores which were relatively large at approximately 2.5mm.

It required the development of some very clever control electronics before magnetic core memory systems could be considered practical and reliable enough to be put into commercial operation.

As we progress through this project you will hopefully appreciate how difficult this task would have been almost 80 years ago.

Figure 1-4 shows an example of a rope core construction.

Figure 1-3 Rope magnetic core memory (ROM)

As the technology developed the number of cores in a memory array rapidly increased and the size of the cores was reduced to much less than 1mm and it was not long before the average core memory contained hundreds of thousands of cores.

There are a number of advantages in minimising the physical size of the cores as not only does this result in more compact memory systems but it also reduces the power required to drive them.
The amount of current passing through the wires in a core which is required to flip the magnetisation state is a function of the volume of the ferrite cores used and so even relatively small reductions in the diameter of a core will reduce its volume by a large percentage with a corresponding reduction in the current required to drive them.
This in turn allows smaller and lower cost drive electronics so the advantages of smaller cores is clear although the down side to small core size is the difficulty in actually assembling the core arrays.
At its peak the core memory manufacturing industry consumed many billions of cores each year.

Figure 1-5 shows a typical magnetic core memory plane with each memory assembly being constructed from many of these planes which were generally arranged in stacks.

In general each plane, or mat, was used to store single bits and the stack was used to store multiple bits of data. For example 8 planes could store 8 bit bytes of information and 16 planes could store 16 bit data values.

Figure 1-4 A single memory plane

This method of construction made the core memory systems very versatile as they could be configured to suit any data word size and so did not restrict designers to systems based on predefined memory arrays of fixed sizes or multiples of 2.

It is very fortunate that this type of memory was incredibly reliable once it had been assembled because repairing or replacing faulty cores would have been extremely difficult. This is especially true in the case of the later systems which used extremely small cores and embedded the finished arrays in resin.

A close up look at one of these planes clearly shows the individual cores which are used to store the individual data bits of data. Figure 1-6 gives a close up view of part of a typical core.

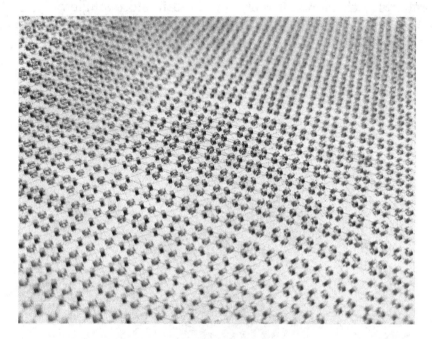

Figure 1-5 Close up view of a typical memory core

Magnetic core memory retained its place as the main data storage technology from the early 1950's until well into the 1970's and was used in some of the best known early computer systems.

One major problem with this type of memory was in actually manufacturing it and from very early in its life there were many attempts to automate the production of core memory but most of these were no more than partly successful. The very success of core memory was largely responsible for the inability of manufacturers to keep up with demand and much of the production was carried out by hand. As I have already indicated the industry consumed billions of cores each year and so it is clear that this technology had a severe limitation.

There was some success in automating the threading of the core mats which was able to reduce the initial wiring of a 64 x 64 mat from over 24 hours to just a few minutes. However as the size of the memory cores continued to shrink the difficulties in fabrication continued to rise.

Magnetic core memory became a victim of its own success by creating a huge demand for ever increasing memory capacity while remaining slow and cumbersome to produce. It is therefore not surprising that it was superseded by silicone chip based solutions which were so much easier to fabricate and could be much more readily scaled up.

It is perhaps worth pointing out that while integrated circuit memory devices transformed computer memory systems they also introduced a whole new set of problems. Moving from highly reliable magnetic core memory to fragile memory devices was not without its problems.

It is interesting to note that most memory cores constructed well over half a century ago still work reliably while anyone involved in vintage computer restoration will be aware that the major failure point in microchip based computer systems is failure of the memory integrated circuits.

Whatever its good and bad points the magnetic core technology was a very important element in the rapid growth of early computer systems and it opened up the possibility for smaller and lower cost computer systems and so was instrumental in the ultimate development of the personal computer which almost everyone relies on today.

In the next chapter we will begin our own journey into core memory development and this will go some way to demonstrate why core memory was always going to be time consuming and expensive to manufacture. Our design will be limited to just a few hundred ferrite cores but the design problems rapidly escalated as the number of cores in the array increased.

It is also worth remembering that we have the advantage of being able to use the information provided to us by history but the original core memory inventors and designers did not have this advantage and had to work out how to implement this technology.

It is unclear how modern computers would have developed without magnetic core memory but it is certain that without it the modern computer would have struggled to become such a universal success.

The development and application of magnetic core memory continued for a considerable time from its initial concepts in the 1940's well into the 1970's and beyond.

Over that time the technology developed significantly in terms of system performance and reduction in cost.

As part of that development process the physical size of the cores shrank and this allowed ever larger core arrays to be implemented.

Not only does making the cores smaller result in a reduction of the magnetic core memory structure size but it also enables the use of less power required to drive the cores.

The power required to change the magnetisation state of a ferrite core is directly related to its volume and the size reduction which took place over the life of the technology allowed the required power to drop to less than 1% of the starting value. That is a major change as it not only reduces the size of the power supplies required but it also reduces the size of the driver circuits.

As you will see later this is one of the most difficult aspects in developing a magnetic core memory system and so anything which can be done to make the system fundamentally less complex is of great assistance.

When I was initially researching this project I would have preferred to select the smaller size of ferrite core as that would have made the development much easier.

However I ended up selecting a mid sized core for a few reasons.

Firstly I wanted the finished design to look interesting because, after all, a large part of the appeal is in the appearance.

I therefore wanted to use cores which were large enough to give an authentic and interesting appearance for the arrays.

The second reason for not selecting the smallest available cores is my ability to actually assemble the arrays with the equipment I have. To give you some idea of the scale involved figure 1-7 shows the range of core sizes which were used between the mid 1940' to the mid 1960's.

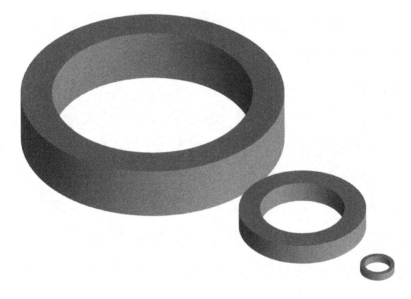

Figure 1-6 Comparison of Core Dimensions

The largest core on the left of the image is the size of core which was originally used in commercial systems and was approximately 2.5mm in diameter.

That is actually quite small but as you can see the cores became very much smaller as the technology matured.

The middle sized core is 1.2mm in diameter and is the size of core which I selected for this project.

It is small enough to be practical to design a system around but large enough to look interesting.

To give a better idea of scale figure 1-8 shows this mid sized core alongside a ballpoint pen tip.

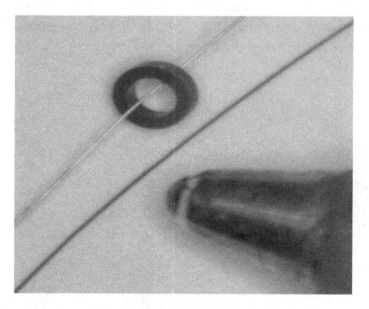

Figure 1-7 Close up View of 1.2mm Ferrite Core

The core on the right in figure 1-7 is the smallest commonly available core which was produced and as you can hopefully see they were incredibly small at around 0.3mm in diameter.

While I could have selected the smaller size for our project I did not like my changes of being able to successfully construct a memory array with such small parts.

As the cores get smaller the size of the wires which can be used is also reduced and this creates even more assembly problems so I decided to use a core with sufficiently large dimensions to increase my chances of success.

I also want to make the bare boards available as a kit so I also considered the ease of assembly for others.

Magnetic Core Logic

Such was the success of magnetic core memory systems that a whole new industry was created and the technology which this industry developed expanded well beyond just memory systems.

There was a whole family of magnetic core logic devices which were able to perform complex logic tasks using specially wound square loop ferrite cores. I will not be discussing these types of devices in this book but wanted to mention them here so that the reader may be prompted to further investigate such technologies once they have reached the end of our development project.

ℰℊℐℰ

Chapter 2 – Principles of operation

Ferrite Properties

Before we start developing a magnetic core memory system we will briefly investigate the properties of the material which we will be using to store the data.

As I stated in the previous chapter this book is intended as a hands on development process in which I will avoid getting heavily involved in the mathematics behind the fundamental physics and material properties. However we will need to take a brief look at the way data will be stored as this will greatly simplify the explanations as we progress through the development of our system.

Should you wish to investigate the theory in more detail then there is a great deal of information available but for the most part I will be skipping over the maths in order to keep us moving forward.

We can begin with a very simply example of an electromagnet and think about what happens when we apply an electrical current to the wire coil of this device.

The electromagnet in this example is simply an iron core around which are wound a number of turns of insulated copper wire.

When current is applied to the copper wire a current starts to flow in this wire and an electromagnetic field is generated around the wire which impinges on the iron core.

As the amplitude of this current rises the electromagnetic field also increases and this in turn causes the magnetic flux within iron core to increase. The more the current increases the stronger the magnetic flux in the core becomes until a point is reached where the magnetic flux is as high as it can get at which point the core is said to be saturated. Trying to increase the field beyond this point will only result in a higher current in the winding but no further increase in the magnetic flux.

If the current in the winding is reduced to the saturation point then further reductions in current will result in a reduction in the magnetic flux and once the current reaches zero the magnetic flux will also be zero.

Actually there will most likely be a residual magnetic flux but we will ignore that for now.

An important property of this electromagnet is that if we apply a rapidly increasing voltage to the coil then the current in the coil will not rise as rapidly as the voltage because the current increase will lag behind the rise in voltage.

This delay in the increase of current in the coil is due to a property of the electromagnetic called inductance and this inductance is a due to the nature of the iron core and the turns of copper wire around it which allow energy to be absorbed by the core.

As the current in the winding tries to increase and generate a magnetic flux in the core the core effectively begins to store energy in its magnetic field (flux) and this has a tendency to resist the increase in current flowing through the winding. As the magnetic field increases then the resistance to current increase reduces and more current can flow in the winding.

When current is removed from the winding the energy stored as a magnetic field in the core begins to collapse and this generates a voltage in the copper winding with current flowing in the opposite direction to the original current which was applied.

So what does this have to do with storing data you may ask and the answer is 'nothing at all' until we replace the iron core.

I mentioned that removing the current flowing through the winding could leave a residual magnetic field but this actually depends on the physical properties of the material used for the core. If we replace the iron core with a ferrite material, which is essentially a mixture of types of finely powdered magnetic material bonded in a specific way, then we can control the properties of the electromagnet in a much more specific manner.

There is a very wide range of ferrite materials with an equally wide range of magnetic properties so we will begin by looking at a ferrite core type which would be used in something such as a transformer.

In a transformer or filter we want the response to changing current and hence changing magnetic field to produce a corresponding change in the magnetic flux in the core. So as the current through the transformer winding increases the magnetic field and hence core flux increases steadily as the current increases and then decreases steadily as the winding current reduces. This should be consistent irrespective of the polarity of the applied current.

Figure 2-1 shows an example of this type of ferrite and clearly shows how the core flux rises and falls in direct response to the changes in the current applied to the winding.

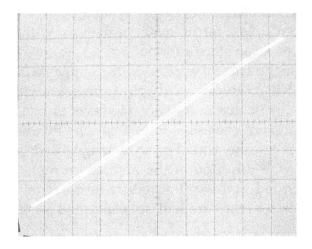

Figure 2-1 'Normal' ferrite material response

It can also be seen that there is a small amount of hysteresis in the response of the core flux so that the change in flux as the applied current decreases does not produce an exact match to the response caused when the current is increasing. It is however consistent for each cycle of applied current and the result is a core which can transfer energy between different windings on the same core.

While this is very useful for transformers and filters it is not much help to us for storing data but other types of ferrite material are available.

Square-Loop Ferrite

For storing data we can turn our attention to the so called 'square-loop ferrite' which looks very similar to the ferrite material suitable for use in transformers and filters but which has some very specific differences in its properties. It is these properties which we will be making use of in the development of our magnetic core memory system.

Unlike the normal ferrite material which we would select for use in transformers the square ferrite variety does not respond in a progressive manner to increasing applied magnetic fields.

If we construct an electromagnet by winding copper wire round a core made from square ferrite material then we will have the basis for a device which can store information.

As we increase the current applied to the copper winding then the magnetic field it produces will begin to increase with a resulting increase in magnetic flux in the core. However unlike normal ferrite the rise in flux is not consistent once a specific flux level is reached and at that point the core becomes magnetised in a direction dependant on the direction of the applied current. If the applied current is then reduced the flux will reduce but once the applied current reaches zero the core will not return to its original state but will remain magnetised.

Should the current then be applied again in the same polarity the magnetic field will increase again in the same direction but this time the core magnetisation will not change because it is already magnetised in the required direction.

The only way that the magnetisation of the core can now be changed is by applying a current to the coil winding in the opposite direction and so a reversed magnetic field is produced. Once the flux induced in the core by this magnetic field reaches a critical level the magnetisation of the core will suddenly be reversed and this direction of magnetisation of the core will remain until the applied current is once again reversed.

It can be seen from this property of square ferrite that it is possible to store information by setting the magnetisation direction in one or more of these cores and so each core can be used to store either a '0' or a '1' depending on the direction of the stored magnetisation.

Figure 2-2 shows a trace using a square loop ferrite core and in this trace the vertical scale represents current and the horizontal scale is the voltage across the inductor wire.

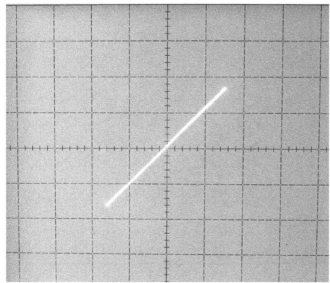

Figure 2-2 Magnetic Filed Below Critical Threshold

The actual vertical scale of this trace is 200mA per division with the centre line at 0mA and an AC current is applied. It can be seen that in this trace the current is varying from +300mA to -300mA but unlike normal ferrite material there is very little out of phase hysterisis so the trace is almost straight.

If we now increase the amplitude of the applied current to +/- 500mA then we start to see deviations in the trace in both the positive phase and the negative phase as shown in the trace in figure 2-3. These deviations start where the current exceeds approximately -350mA and +350mA. That figure is important so make a mental note of it because we will be coming back to it later in the book.

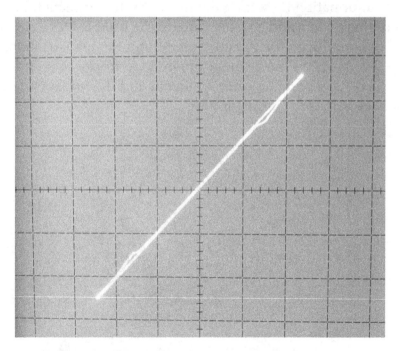

Figure 2-3 Current at Threshold

If we continue to increase the amplitude of the applied current then the magnitude of the deviations also increases although the current at which they occur does not change and again that is an important characteristic which we will return to later.

Figure 2-4 shows a trace in which the magnitude of the applied current is far greater than the critical threshold for the ferrite core being used. It is important to understand that the actual current at which these transitions occur is entirely dependant on the particular ferrite core and the core used in this case is the type we will be using in our memory system.

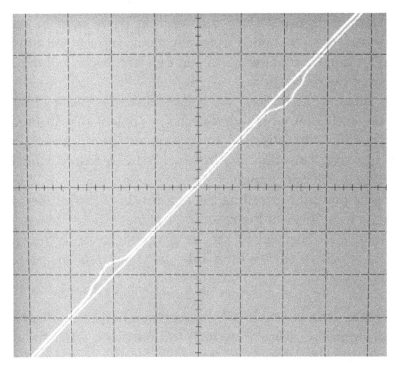

Figure 2-4 Applied Current Higher than Critical Threshold

Another important thing to mention here is that the deviations we are seeing in the traces only occur when an AC current is applied.

If we only apply a current in one polarity then we will only see a deviation in the first cycle, assuming that the core is magnetised in the opposing direction, and for subsequent cycles the trace would be a flat line.

These deviations in the traces are caused when the ferrite core flips magnetisation state and this is the key characteristic which core memory makes use of.

So the next question we must answer is how we can make use of the unusual 'square' response property of this ferrite material in order to build a working memory storage unit.

If we examine figure 2-4 we can see that if we only increase the applied current, and hence magnetic field, by a small amount in either direction then nothing will happen irrespective of the current direction of magnetisation.

As the current increases we will eventually reach the critical magnetic field level which generates a sufficient flux in the core to force the core magnetisation to change to the required direction unless the magnetisation is already in the required direction in which case it will not change.

This means that by controlling the amplitude of the applied current and so the total level of the resulting magnetic field we can build a system that can be used to set the magnetic core to the required direction which in turn will enable us to set a '0' or a '1' as we require.

We now have the ability to set the core magnetisation direction but we also require a means by which to determine what the existing magnetisation direction is so that we are able to read the stored value. If we now look at the response of the core to the applied magnetic field we can easily see a means by which this can be accomplished.

I use the word 'easily' here but as you will see it is far from a simple task to design a system capable of detecting the flux states.

Whenever the core changes its magnetisation state the flux goes through a very rapid transition and this will generate a rapid current spike in any winding on the core and it is this spike which is used to determine the current direction of magnetisation in the core.

We can assume that the required data value is already saved in the core and so all we now need to do is read that value back.

By applying a sufficiently high current to the winding to create a magnetic field strong enough to flip the core magnetisation direction we can determine is the core is storing a '0' or a '1'.

Let us assume that the magnetic field we are applying is trying to flip the core magnetisation from a '1' to a '0' then if we are able to detect a spike in our core winding then we know that the core had a '1' stored but if no spike is detected then we know that nothing changed and so the core was storing a '0'.

While this works it has a major flaw which is that it is a destructive read because it will result in the core ending up with a stored value of '0' irrespective of its original value.

There is of course an easy solution to this which is to write the value we read from the core back into the core following each read. This will restore the original data value following the read although it does mean that every read will be a two step process of a read followed by a write. There are times when writing the value back to the core is not required but we will ignore such advanced operation for now and assume that we always want to perform non destructive reads.

We now have almost everything we need to begin designing our magnetic core memory system. I say almost because there is one more key element which we will need in order to create a useful memory system.

So far we have only considered a single bit of data storage but for a practical data storage system we will of course require far more storage capacity and a way to explicitly access any locations within the memory array.

The method most often used to provide this functionality was the so called coincidence current and inhibit system. We have already seen that a minimum level of magnetic field is required in order to cause the flux in the memory ferrite core to become high enough to flip the magnetisation of the core. It can be noted here that the strength of the magnetic field and hence the magnetic flux in any given ferrite core is the sum of the magnetic fields created by all the windings on that particular core.

With that in mind if we pass two wires through a single core we can pass a current through one of those wires which will produce approximately 60% of the magnetic field strength which would cause the core magnetisation to change state. If the current was then removed there would be no lasting change in the state of the core magnetisation. However if we pass the same current through both of the wires which we passed through the core then the resulting sum of the magnetic fields produced by the two wires would be sufficient to cause the core magnetisation to change state.

From this we can determine that by arranging the cores in a two dimensional grid such that a separate single wire passes through all the cores in each horizontal row and a separate single wire passes though all the cores in each vertical column then we would have the ability to individually address individual cores in such a way that individual core magnetic fields can be taken above the required core transition threshold without affecting other cores in the same grid.

For example if we had an 8x8 grid of magnetic cores and identified each row as X0 to X7 and each column as Y0 to Y7 then we could access the core at location X3,Y5 (for example) by driving row X3 and column Y5 with the 60% of the critical current.

This would produce a sufficiently strong magnetic field in the core at location X3,Y5 to force its core magnetisation to change state, assuming that it was not already in the required state.

While other cores in the X3 row would see the 60% magnetic field this would not be sufficient for their magnetisation to change state and the same is true of the other cores in the Y5 column. Only the core at location X3,Y5 would change state and that is exactly what we want.

We can then arrange as many of these arrays so that we have one for each data bit we wish to store. For example if we wanted to store 8 bit values then we would use 8 of these 8x8 arrays to give us a total storage capacity of 64 x 8 bit bytes.

This is in fact the layout which I intend to use and while this may be a tiny amount of data storage by modern computer standards it is still enough to give us a useable amount of memory to create a simple test computer and is also enough to create design problems. Figure 2-5 shows the arrangement for a single array.

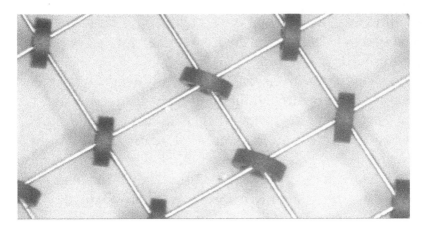

Figure 2-5 Single memory core array

Figure 2-6 shows an assembled core memory array board.

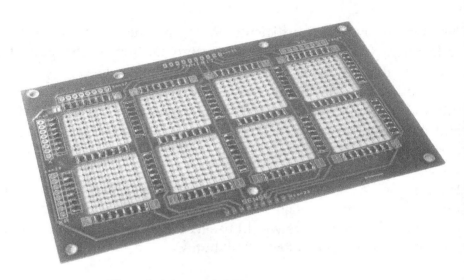

Figure 2-6 Assembled Memory Array Board

We now have a mechanism which we can use to set any combination of data bits in our 64 bit arrays but there is still a problem to solve which is how to avoid setting bits to a '1' when we want to leave them set to a '0'.

The solution to this problem is also relatively simple and can easily be achieved by adding a third wire to our array which is referred to as the 'Inhibit' line.

A separate inhibit wire is passed through every core in each 8x8 array so we end up with 8 inhibit lines, one for each array.

We have already determined that to set an individual core magnetisation we simply need to apply current to both the X and the Y wires passing through that core. However if we do not want to cause that core magnetisation to flip then we can simply apply a 60% current to the inhibit wire but in the opposite direction to the X and Y drive currents. As the total magnetic field created is the sum of the fields produced by all the currents flowing through all the wires which pass through the core then we will then have +60% + 60% -60% and this will result in the same magnetic field as only passing current through a single X or Y wire.

This is because the current in the inhibit wire will cancel the magnetic field created by one of the other two wires. This means that the magnetic field is only 60% of the level required to cause the core magnetisation to flip and so we can now use a combination of X and Y currents along with inhibit currents to set any combination of core states that we desire.

It is important to understand at this point that we do not explicitly set bits to '0' when we write data to the memory but instead we will 'clear' all the bits to a '0' and then set all bits to a '1' which need to be set and we will use the inhibit wires to prevent setting the bits which need to remain at '0'.

We can now set any combination of data in the arrays that we want but we now need a way to actually read the data out of the arrays. As already stated previously the rapid change in flux which occurs when a core changes magnetisation state will induce a current spike in any wire passing through that particular core. We can therefore design a means to read the core values by duplicating the arrangement of the inhibit lines by passing a wire through every core in each 8x8 array so we end up with 8 sense lines, one for each array.

To read a data byte from memory all we now need to do is to select the 8 bits, one from each 8x8 array for a given memory address by passing a current through the select lines but in the opposite direct to that used to write the data values into memory. This will cause any cores with a magnetisation direction which represents a '1' to be forced to flip to the '0' direction.

For example if we select the location X3,Y5 from all 8 arrays then any of the selected 8 cores which contained a '1' will be flipped to a '0' and a current spike will be induced in the sense line for the affected 8x8 arrays.

Any cores which were already at '0' will not cause a spike in their sense lines.

By monitoring the sense lines during the read process at the correct time we can determine the data value that was stored at the selected memory location.

At this point we have of course deleted the data because this process forces all the cores to a '0' state but as long as we include suitable logic steps required to write the data value we have read back into the same memory location then we will have a fully functional memory system.

In this explanation I have described a system which has four wires passing through each memory core which are the X and Y selection lines and a sense and inhibit line. However most commercial systems developed used a combined inhibit and sense line as this greatly simplified the production of the memory core assemblies by removing the need for one of the wires and the only penalty was more complex control electronics but as the electronics only needed to be designed once this was easier than having to include the additional wire in the hard to manufacture cores.

Using a single wire for both the inhibit and sense functions is a lot easier than it may first sound because when we consider the operation of the system as described above it can be seen that the inhibit wire is only used during a write cycle and the sense wire is only used during a read cycle so they are never used at the same time.

However to keep the explanations as clear as possible I will begin with separate inhibit and sense wires although our final design will use a common sense and inhibit wire which I will describe in a later chapter.

It should be noted here that assembling the memory array boards is fairly challenging due to the small dimensions of the cores but it is no impossible although a microscope is recommend. I will be providing some guidance on assembling an array board in a later chapter.

Figure 2-7 Partially Assembled Memory Array Board

Because the operation of the core is entirely dependent on the current polarities flowing in the core wires I thought that it was worth repeating this information again.

The following diagrams should also help to clarify exactly what we are looking for in our design and should assist in determining the way in which we need to connect the array wires to the current drivers.

Although we will be using a 3 wire design for our ferrite core array it is easier to visualise the requirements if we assume that 4 wires will be used. Just remember that we will be combining the Sense and Inhibit functions into a single wire but these diagrams will also show why we can easily do that.

Read Operation Current Polarities

Figure 2-8 shows the current directions flowing in the core wires during a read operation. Note that the diagrams show the cases for when the ferrite core is having its magnetisation state changed but for cases where passing additional current pulses of the same polarity through the same wires will result in no changes to the memory cores.

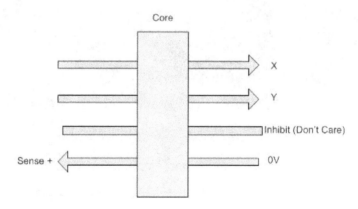

Figure 2-8 Read Current Polarities

In figure 2-8 we can see that currents are flowing in both the X and the Y selection wires and so the total combined current will generate a magnetic field which is strong enough the cause the ferrite core to change state.

This has the effect of inducing a signal pulse in the sense wire for any cores which actually change state and these are the cores which were storing a data value which we are calling '1'.

Any cores which do not change state will not produce any sense wire output and so we assume that those cores were storing a data value of '0'.

During a read operation we simply ignore the inhibit wire as it is not needed although we must be sure not to pass a current through it or the core data values may be corrupted.

Write Operation Current Polarities

Figure 2-9 shows the current directions flowing in the core wires during a write operation. Note that the diagrams show the cases for when the ferrite core is having its magnetisation state changed but for cases where passing additional current pulses of the same polarity through the same wires will result in no changes to the memory cores as in the read cycle.

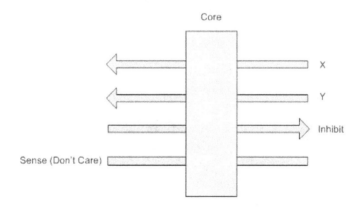

Figure 2-9 Write Current Polarities

For our system to operate correctly we must create a set of circuits which can provide the carefully timed and shaped current pulses to the correct array wires. We must also ensure that the current pulses in each wire are of the correct polarity for each phase of the read and write memory cycles.

The response from the ferrite cores is also time dependant and so our design must take that into account to ensure that we obtain reliable and consistent results from the system.

While this all sounds like a difficult design process I hope to show that by breaking the development down into various steps and sub systems that it can be easily completed.

I also hope to demonstrate some simple project development techniques which I hope may be of use to the reader if they are not already conversant with systems design.

For the general hobbyist the approach to project management is of no real practical consequence although a carefully considered design philosophy can still prove useful. For professional development engineers and in particular engineers who manage larger projects then good resource management is very important and can make the difference between a successful development and one which either fails or runs out of control making it too costly to complete.

I will keep this project as simple and clear as possible by stepping through the design in what I hope will be logical steps and for anyone already familiar with the development process I hope that the nature of the technology will still make this process interesting.

ℒℱℒ

Chapter 3 – Selecting a Suitable Ferrite Core

Testing cores and characterising for design

In the last chapter I briefly described how our magnetic core memory will work and I am sure it is obvious that a key to the operation of this type of memory system are the characteristics of the ferrite cores. It is therefore important that we choose ferrite cores which have properties suitable for our intended design.

The memory system I will be presenting in this book will most certainly not be a high performance machine but even so the cores we select will have a major bearing on the success of this project. I have already stated that I will be starting with a 4 wire design rather than the more usual 3 wire designs which were most common in typical magnetic core memory systems.

I will also not be implementing the so called core discharge features which are intended to improve high speed performance of these circuits although I will describe their operation in later chapters.

For our basic design there are just a few core characteristics we will need to concern ourselves with and the first one of these is more of a practical consideration rather than a technical one. That characteristic is the physical size of the cores we will be using as I will need to be able to manually construct the core with wires that are strong enough to allow relatively easy core threading. The larger the cores then the easier they will be to handle but this leads to two secondary considerations. The fist of these is the least important and is the final assembled size of our memory arrays.

Each of the arrays will have 8x8 or 64 cores and we will have a total of 8 arrays to give a grand total of 512 cores and while this may be a very small number of cores compared to a commercially assembled core it is still a sufficiently high number to result in a very large and cumbersome design if large cores are used.

The second consideration is much more important and it is due to the fact that the amount of energy we must apply to a core in order to flip its magnetisation state is a function of the core volume and so even a modest increase in core diameter will result in a large increase in the amount of energy we would need to apply. This would in turn require large and powerful drivers and hence large power supplies along with numerous other complications if we tried to drive large amounts of power into highly inductive loads. It is therefore important that the cores we select are as small as possible while still allowing us to actually assemble the core and even then it is almost certain that this work will need to be carried out with the assistance of a microscope.

Before we start designing the core array structure we will carry out a few empirical tests on the cores which we intend to use in this design.

The core I have selected for this design is the 5221.3-2113.35 and while these are very large by typical standards at approximately 1.2mm outside diameter they are still small enough to allow operation using reasonably manageable currents. The hole in this size of core is also big enough to allow reasonably large diameter wires to be used and this will provide good support for the finished structure. They are also large enough so that the finished core will look interesting and while that may not be of any significant practical value it is still worthy of mention.

For our design to work successfully we will need to determine the magnetic field required to generate a sufficiently high flux density needed to cause the core to change state. The level we select will not only determine the flux transitions but also the sense signal amplitude which will be produced by these transitions.

We will then set our current generators at a fixed percentage of this value as indicated in the previous chapter but we must of course determine the current required in the selection wires to generate the required magnetic field and there are several ways we can do this.

For our practical approach we will discover this value empirically by driving a number of cores at various levels until we have been able to determine the nominal current we need to use.

Before we start testing a real ferrite core it may be a good idea to expand a little on the behaviour of the 'square-loop' ferrite material in order that we can more clearly interpret our test results.

I gave a brief description earlier as to how this material responds to applied magnetic field but we need to know a little more before we begin our actual design.

For the sake of this explanation we can ignore the means by which a magnetic field is actually applied to the ferrite core and for now just concentrate on the effect that this magnetic field has on the magnetic flux of the ferrite core itself.

If we begin by taking a square-loop ferrite core which has never seen a magnetic field before then it will not have any stored magnetic field and so its stored magnetic flux value can be said to be zero.

In practice the cores will generally already have a stored magnetic flux but this does not affect the measurements we need to make and once the memory system is constructed we will actually make use of the residual stored flux.

However for the sake of explanation we can assume that our test core starts with no stored flux at all and look at what happens once a magnetic field is applied. The actual initial response from a totally flux free core will not be exactly the same as from a core with a stored flux but this is of no practical concern to us as our memory cores will all have stored flux the first time we use them.

Figure 3-1 shows the relationship between the applied magnetic field and the magnetic flux within the core as the applied magnetic field is varied.

It is important to understand that this diagram shows the behaviour when the magnitude of the applied magnetic field is always below what we will describe as the *critical threshold*.

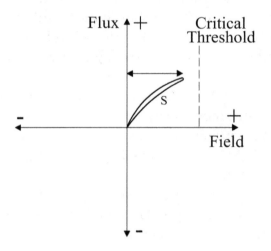

Figure 3-1 Un-polarised Magnetic core

In this diagram the X axis represents the magnitude of the magnetic field which is being applied to the ferrite core and the Y axis represents the level of the magnetic flux which is induced into the ferrite core.

For the sake of explanation we will define the magnetic field as increasing in a positive sense towards the right of the diagram and having a value of zero in the centre of the diagram and increasing in a negative sense towards the left of the diagram.

In the same way we will represent the magnitude of the flux within the core as increasing from zero in the centre of the diagram in a positive sense towards the top of the diagram and increasing in a negative sense towards the bottom of the diagram.

The use of positive and negative values in this context is purely arbitrary but as long as we are consistent then it will help with the explanation.

In figure 3-1 we can see that as the applied magnetic field is varied from zero to a relatively small positive value then the flux in the core changes in a corresponding way so it appears to be behaving in a similar manner to normal ferrite material. The response curve is shown by the line labelled 'S'.

It is important to appreciate that this behaviour is only consistent as long as the applied magnetic field remains below the critical threshold which is shown on the diagram by the vertical dotted line.

Things get much more interesting if the applied magnetic field is increased to a level which exceeds the critical threshold and the effect of this is shown in Figure 3-2.

Once the applied magnetic field strength exceeds the critical threshold, indicated by 'T' in the diagram, then something interesting happens to the ferrite core. The core itself becomes magnetised and so it effectively stores the magnetic flux.

Reducing the applied magnetic field once this has happened no longer causes the core flux to return to zero but to retain the majority of the flux value that it acquired when the magnetic field was present.

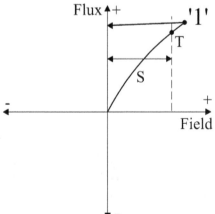

Figure 3-2 Flipping the Magnetisation

In figure 3-2 the flux value retained by the ferrite core when the applied magnetic field was in the positive direction is shown as storing a data value of '1' but again this is entirely arbitrary and it is up to us as the designers to determine what it actually means.

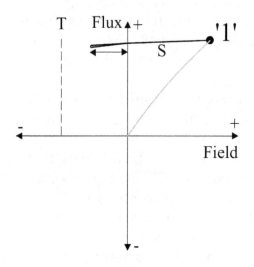

Figure 3-3 Magnetisation hysteresis

Now that the core has stored a particular flux value it can retain that stored flux even if a magnetic field is reapplied as shown in Figure 3-3

In figure 3-3 it can be seen that if the applied magnetic field is increased again in the positive direction, even past the previous critical threshold then nothing will change and the flux will remain at its stored '1' state and will remain at that level when the applied magnetic field is once again reduced to zero. In fact we can now assume that the critical threshold is no longer on the right side of the diagram but has now moved to the left side of the diagram as shown by the dotted line 'T'. If we now vary the applied magnetic field in the negative direction as shown in figure 3-3 then the resulting flux will tend to remain unchanged as long as the applied magnetic field does not exceed the critical threshold.

Clearly we have successfully stored a value of '1' in our magnetic core.

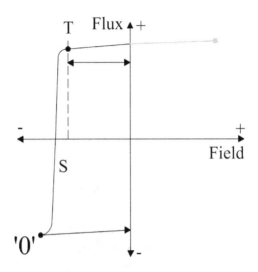

Figure 3-4 Flipping the magnetisation again

Things now get more interesting if the applied magnetic field now exceeds the critical threshold (T) and figure 3-4 shows the results of this. Once the critical threshold has been exceeded then the flux in the ferrite core suddenly flips polarity and becomes magnetised in the opposite direction and that is designated in figure 3-4 as representing a data value of '0'.

The new '0' flux value is retained even once the applied magnetic field is reduced to a value of zero.

Furthermore the stored flux value will be retained if the applied magnetic field level exceeds the critical threshold in the negative direction although once again we can now assume that the critical threshold is back towards the right side of the diagram.

The stored flux value will also be retained if we vary the applied magnetic field in the positive direction as long as we do not exceed the critical threshold 'T' as shown in figure 3-5.

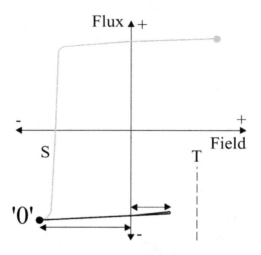

Figure 3-5 Magnetisation hysterisis again

If the applied magnetic field strength now exceeds the critical threshold then the ferrite core flux will once again suddenly change state and the magnetisation will be reversed so that it reverts back to storing the flux value which represents a data value of '1'.
This change can be seen in figure 3-6 and we have now completed our journey around the square loop of the ferrite property curve.

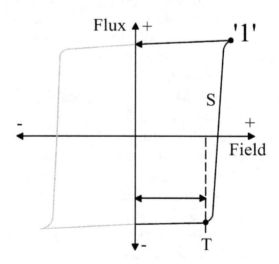

Figure 3-6 Completing the Magnetisation loop

We can continue to modify the stored flux state by simply applying a magnetic field of sufficient amplitude and in the correct direction depending on the flux state that we want to store. Once we have driven a particular core into one state or the other then it will always be storing either a '0' or a '1' and we can determine which and this in turn allows us to use this mechanism to store data.

This is of course only half of the story as we still need a means by which we can read back the stored data value. A memory system which required us to remember the state of the stored values would hardly be of much use to us.

The key to this part of the problem is to think about what happens in a conductor which is subject to a rapidly changing magnetic field.

In the previous explanation is stated that the core flux will rapidly change from a '0' state to a '1' state under certain conditions and from a '1' state to a '0' state under different conditions and it is that sudden change of state that we can use to read back the stored state. All we need to do is pass a wire through the core and use it to detect the changes in the magnetisation state of the core flux.

Whenever the magnetic field changes around a conductor a current is induced in that conductor which is proportional to the rate of change of the magnetic field.

The rapid change in flux caused when the ferrite core changes state as the critical threshold is passed causes a current to be generated in the 'sense' wire which we have passed through the core.

This current is relatively small but we can easily amplify it and use the resulting signal to determine what the state of the core was.

Figure 3-7 gives an example of what this may look like and it can be seen that if the core flux changes from a '1' to a '0' during the read process then a signal will be detected but any cores which are already set to '0' will not produce any output.

Unfortunately the action of reading the data is destructive and results in all the addressed cores ending up with a flux status for a '0' value.

However as we have just read out the data value which was stored in the cores we can easily write this data back into the cores.

As part of our initial testing we will need to determine how to go about amplifying the signals on the sense wires in addition to measuring the required drive currents which we will need to use to properly control the memory cores.

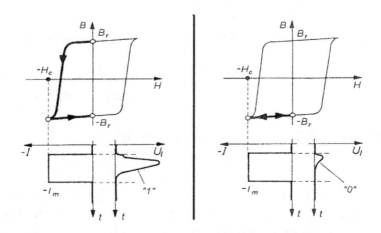

Figure 3-7 Ferrite flip output

We now have enough information to begin testing our actual ferrite cores and the aim of this testing is to determine the total core selection conductor current which is required in order to switch the magnetisation of the selected core.

We also need to measure the signal output in the core sense wire so that we can design a suitable sense amplifier.

Once we have determined the nature of the signal we can expect from the output of the core sense wire we can more easily design a suitable amplifier circuit and for a system like this the sense amplifier is a critical part of the overall design and system performance.

During initial testing we must also bear in mind that our system requires a large number of circuits so careful design is important.

In order to perform this testing I needed to configure a single core in such a manner that I could measure the required characteristics and figure 3-8 shows the setup I used for this.

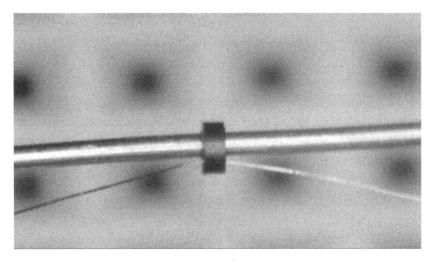

Figure 3-8 Ferrite Core Test Rig

This setup consists of a single core with two wires passed through it with the thicker wire connected to a pulse current source and the thinner wire connected to an oscilloscope.

The pulse generator will pass a single pulse of current from an adjustable constant current source through the thick 'selection' wire and we can adjust the pulse width and peak current.

We can then observer the signal induced into the thinner 'sense' wire to determine the point at which the magnetic filed produced is sufficient to cause the core magnetisation to flip.

As I previously described this should cause a sudden change in magnetic flux which will in turn induce a current into the sense wire and we should see this as a voltage spike on the oscilloscope.

The output signal will be very small and of short duration so gathering data from a large number of tests will be the best approach.

As with most electronic development projects there are a few complications we must deal with before we can get started on the core tests.

As stated above the testing will consist of applying pulses of current into the selection wire which is running through the core shown in figure 3-8. Unfortunately this will produce some unwanted effects which we will need to deal with if the final memory system is to work reliably.

The main problem we will encounter when we apply a current pulse to the conductor is that what we have actually assembled in figure 3-8 is a transformer with 2 winding's, each winding has a single turn of course. This means that when we apply a pulse to one of these windings then a current will be induced in the second winding. In this case we are applying the current pulse to the selection winding and so a corresponding pulse will be created in the sense winding. Although we could simply choose to ignore the pulse which is generated by arranging the timing of the various signals it is certainly not ideal to have this secondary current pulse because it will interfere with our ability to detect the actual signals we are looking for. The required timing to avoid this pulse will also be highly dependant on the characteristics of the core assembly and so it will be unpredictable and would make finding a reliable solution very difficult. It is therefore much more preferable for us to find a method which will eliminate this secondary pulse instead of simply trying to avoid it.

Figure 3-9 shows the result of applying a pulse to the selection wire and as we can see the current creates a rapidly changing magnetic flux which the core couples to the sense wire. The top trace is the applied current and the bottom trace is the resulting signal in the sense wire.

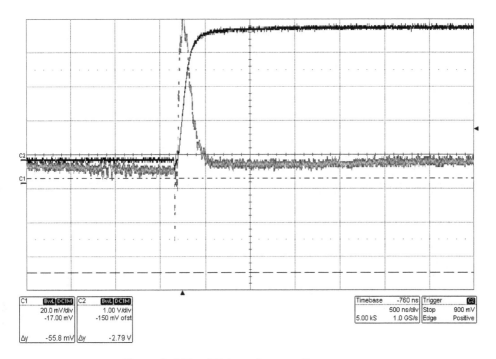

Figure 3-9 Fast Rising edge coupling response

It is clear in figure 3-9 that the signal induced in the sense wire is a result of the rapidly changing current in the selection wire and it is in fact the rate of change of current in the selection wire which is responsible for the magnitude of the secondary signal.

We will of course encounter a similar problem if we reverse the current in the selection wire and apply a pulse in the opposite direction and the effect of this can be seen in figure 3-10.

The magnitude and position of these secondary pulses will vary depending on the nature of the magnetic memory core assembly and so anything we can do to reduce this effect will be beneficial to our final design. This problem will also rapidly increase as the size of the memory core increases and so eliminating it now will make further development of the system in future much more straight forward.

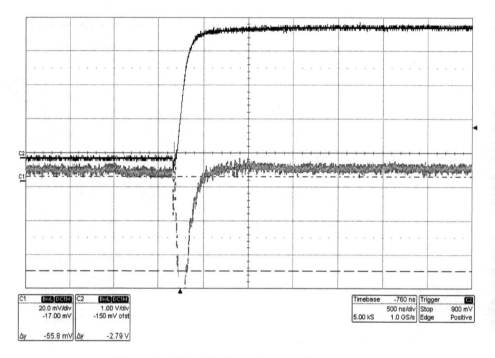

Figure 3-10 Fast Falling edge coupling response

To further clarify why these secondary pulses would make designing around them difficult figure 3-11 shows how the sense wire output signal would look in the presence of an actual data pulse.

In these diagrams the top current trace is showing a current pulse magnitude of approximately 650mA and the signal from the sense wire peaks at less than 100mV and so the nature of the design problem is fairly significant.

As we can see the dual secondary pulse would make reliable detection of the intended data pulse difficult or even impossible depending on the core structure characteristics and in fact the actual output signal we need to detect will be very much lower amplitude than the signal we are observing here.

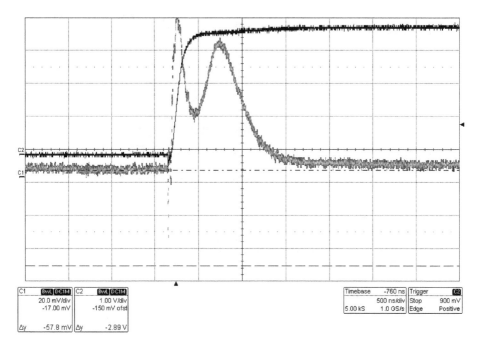

Figure 3-11 Magnetisation switch pulse output

Fortunately there is a simple solution to this problem because the current induced in the sense wire is directly related to the rate of change of current in the selection wire.

This implies that all we need to do in order to eliminate, or at least reduce the impact of the secondary pulse is to control the rate of change of current in the selection wire.

If we slow the rate at which the current changes in the selection wire then the result will be to reduce the current induced in the sense wire. There is a limit how much we can slow down the selection current pulse because the memory system is expected to operate at a relatively fast rate and so any delays we introduce will slow the overall operation of the system.

Figure 3-12 shows the effect of slowing the selection current pulse rising edge and figure 3-13 shows the same for a reversed current.

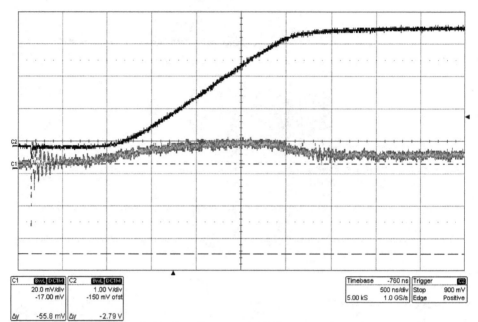

Figure 3-12 Coupling output with slow rising edge

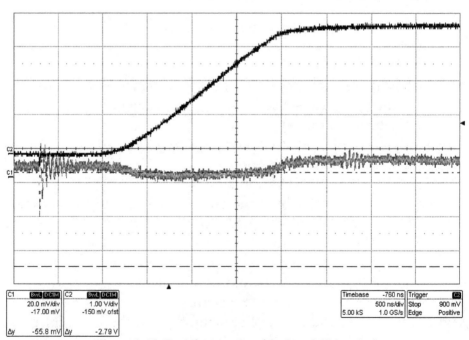

Figure 3-13 Coupling output with slow falling edge

In figure 3-12 and figure 3-13 we can see how the selection current pulse leading edge has been slowed from its original 200nS to around 2uS. This in turn has greatly reduced the amplitude of the signal in the sense wire and the actual goal here is to bring the signal produced by the leading edge of the selection pulse to a level which is significantly lower than the expected signal pulse. As we can see in the diagrams the amplitude of the sense wire signal due to the selection pulse is now down to around 10mV.

A secondary benefit in slowing the selection pulse edge is that the timing of the output signal from the sense wire will now be much more predictable and much less dependant on the structure of the memory core. This is because a slow rising edge will be affected to a much smaller degree by variations in the core characteristics than a rapidly changing signal would be.

Although this technique will work very well in reducing the direct coupled signal I will actually be using a different method in the final design. It is however very convenient to carry out the initial tests using slope control in order that we can more reliably determine the response of the magnetic core as it switches flux states.

Sense Output Detection

Now that we can apply a selection current pulse without generating large unwanted signals we can start looking at the actual signal pulses in the sense wire which are caused by the changes in the magnetisation state of the cores.

Figure 3-14 shows the signal from the sense wire when we apply a current to the selection wire which causes the core magnetisation to flip states. As there is now no longer an unwanted pulse preceding the signal which we are looking for then our job in designing a circuit to detect this signal will be much less complicated.

Figure 3-15 shows the sense wire signal when the core flips states in the opposite direction.

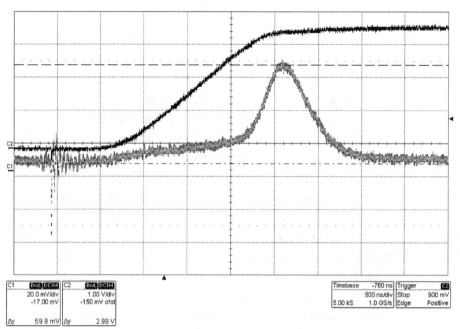

Figure 3-14 Magnetisation switch with slow rising current

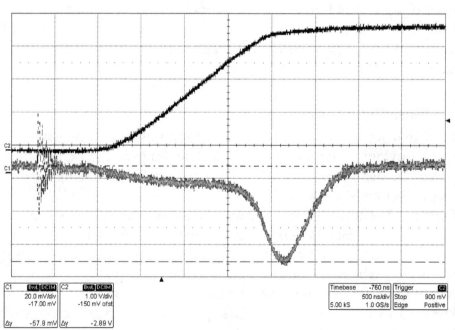

Figure 3-15 Magnetisation switch with slow falling current

Now that we can reliably identify the wanted signal output pulses we need to determine the current level which is required in the selection wire to generate a sufficiently strong magnetic field in order force the ferrite core to flip magnetisation states.

The first step in testing is to slowly increase the magnitude of the selection pulses until we reach the point where the core starts to respond.

During these tests a short pulse of known current is applied to the selection wire and the output from the sense wire is captured on the scope. Remember that once a core has flipped magnetisation states then no further output signals will be seen in the sense wire until the current flowing in the selection wire is reversed.

Note that this will also reverse the polarity of the output pulse in the sense wire although in normal operation we will only be interested in one polarity of output signal. For now however we will reverse the selection current each time the ferrite core flips magnetisation state and repeat the tests.

After each current pulse is applied we can examine the signals captured by the scope to determine if the core flipped state. If the core did flip state then we will see a signal output such as that displayed in figure 3-14 or figure 3-15 depending on the polarity of the magnetic field. If the core did not flip state then no output signal will be seen as shown in figure 3-12 or figure 3-13 again depending on the polarity of the current passing through the selection wire.

By varying the magnitude of the current pulse applied to the selection wire we can determine the current which is required to cause the ferrite core to flip. It should be noted that the amplitude of the output signal on the sense wire will depend on the magnitude of the current flowing in the selection wire and so this current not only needs to be high enough to cause the core to flip magnetisation state but it also must be large enough to produce an output signal of sufficient amplitude to be reliably detected.

We must also however bear in mind that the memory operates on the current coincidence principle which we will come back to shortly.

I performed a large number of tests on a representative selection of the ferrite cores in which I applied a wide range of current pulses to each test core and averaged these results which are show in table 1.

Table 1
Ferrite core test results

Current Applied	Output Signal
100mA	None
150mA	None
200mA	None
250mA	None
300mA	None
350mA	None
400mA	5mV
450mA	10mV
500mA	17mV
550mA	34mV
600mA	49mV
650mA	68mV
700mA	79mV

We already know that the signal level induced by direct coupling between the selection wire and the sense wire is approximately 10mV when we use a pulse with a slow rising edge so we require a signal level which is significantly higher than 10mV if we are to have a system which can reliably detect the output pulses generated when a core flips magnetisation state. The system also needs to be able to correctly determine when the signal level indicates that a core did not change states.

From table 1 we can see that at a current magnitude of 550mA or higher the output signal level exceeds 30mV and so this will be easy to differentiate from the unwanted signal level.

Coincidence Principle

We now come to one of the very clever aspects of a magnetic core memory system and that is the coincidence current principle which the system uses to allow addressing of individual cores. Without the ability to address individual cores the magnetic core memory system would have been much less useful as it would need separate circuitry to control each core within the memory array and so no advantage would be gained by using magnetic cores to store data.

Remember that the magnetisation state of a ferrite core can be flipped by applying a sufficiently strong magnetic field to it as long as the direction of the magnetic field opposes the existing core magnetisation state.

In the testing I have carried out so far the selection current, as shown in table 1, was passed through a single conductor in order to produce the required magnetic field.

However it does not matter if we pass a current of known magnitude through a single conductor or half that current through two conductors. As long as both conductors pass through the core and the currents flow in the same relative direction then the resulting magnetic field amplitude will be the same.

We can therefore divide the total current required to produce the required magnetic field by 2 and use 2 conductors to achieve the same magnetic field but where things get clever is in using one of these two wires for the X selection current and the second wire for the Y selection current.

The result of doing this is that only cores where the X and Y selection wires pass through the same core will have a total combined, or coincidence, current to produce a magnetic field strong enough to cause the ferrite core to flip magnetisation state, assuming that it was not already in the target state.

The same wires can pass through other cores but only the cores with sufficient combined magnetic fields will change state.

If we now go back to table 1 we can see that if we select a current of 350mA for a single selection wire then this will be insufficient on its own to cause any cores to change state. However if two wires carrying 350mA pass through the same core with the current flowing in the same direction then the total effective current will be 700mA which will easily provide a magnetic field which is strong enough to cause the ferrite core to flip magnetisation state.

This now gives us the ability to selectively change the state of any core in an X, Y grid arrangement and if we arrange a number of such grids into a single structure then we have the basis for a data storage system.

Inhibit Action

One final point I will repeat here is that we still need a way to prevent cores from changing state if we want them to remain in their 'un-flipped' state.

This is where the inhibit wire comes into action.

If we assume that we already have the X and Y wires passing though a single core and each has a current of 350mA flowing through it then this would be sufficient to cause the core to change state. Adding another wire which we will call the 'inhibit' wire through the same core allows us to then pass a current through this inhibit wire but in the opposite direction to the currents flowing in the X and Y selection wires.

The result of this is the same as the net product of the currents flowing in all three wires and so we have:

Effective Net Current = 350mA + 350mA - 350mA = 350mA

This is assuming we use the same level of current in the inhibit wire but in the opposite polarity.

The net result of this is effectively a current of just 350mA which as we can see in table 1 is not sufficient to cause the core to flip state.

We can use the three wires in any core mat to determine what the state of any individual core will be if we assume that they are start with the same polarity of magnetisation state.

This is the principle on which a magnetic core memory system works and so our design job is clear. We must create a system which is capable of applying the required current levels to the correct memory cores and then be able to read back the magnetisation state of these cores.
This is the system we will develop throughout the remainder of this book.
Although I will explain the operation of the magnetic core memory system in more detail in later chapters I will briefly explain its operation sequence here so that we know what we are aiming for.

Memory Write

To write data into the memory we must decode the supplied memory address so that we can select the appropriate set of memory cores based on their X and Y positions in each memory array mat. For our system that will be 8 cores with one selected in each array mat.

We then erase all memory cores in those locations to the zero (0) state. This step is required because we will only be actively writing the one (1) bits to the cores and inhibiting the state change of any cores which need to store a zero (0) bit value.

We then use the data in the incoming data bus buffer to enable the inhibit line on any mat where its selected core should remain at a zero (0) state and leave the inhibit lines un-selected for any mats where the selected core state will need to be flipped to represent a one (1).

Finally we apply a selection pulse of controlled rate and amplitude to the decoded X and Y selection lines.

The result will be flipping the magnetisation state of the selected cores where a one (1) needs to be stored and leaving cores unchanged where a zero (0) needs to be stored.

Memory Read

To perform a memory read we must begin by decoding the supplied memory address so that we can select the appropriate set of memory cores based on their X and Y positions in each memory array mat. For our system that will be 8 cores with one selected in each array mat.

Then we apply a selection pulse of controlled rate and amplitude to the decoded X and Y selection lines and at the correct time we also strobe the sense line amplifier outputs so that the data which was stored in the selected memory cores is transferred into the memory read buffer.

Because the above process has the effect of setting all the selected memory cores to the zero (0) state then we must now write the value currently stored in the memory read buffer (the value we have just read) back into the same memory cores we just read the data from. We do this using the same sequence as for a normal memory write described above except that we select the source data from the memory read buffer instead of the incoming data buffer.

Finally we enable the data output latch buffer so that the data currently in the memory read buffer is available on the external data bus.

While it would of course be easy to perform all of the above actions and sequences using a modern microcontroller I made the decision early in this project that I would be using TTL devices and discrete components in the design as this will be far more in keeping with the magnetic core memory technology and it will also be fun.

The overall system design can be conceptually divided into three major elements and this will make development of the system much easier.

If we try to design a system without breaking it down into separate operational blocks then the overall system design could become over complicated.

The way I will be approaching the design of this system is to create separate electronic sub systems for the following parts of the memory system.

Selection Wire Drivers – Convert logic input to wire drive currents

Sense Amplifier and Inhibit Drivers – Sense output signals

Control Logic – Signal sequencing and interfacing circuits.

Each of these elements will be designed separately and by taking this approach each part can be designed without needing to compromise their operation.

The first step in our system design is the development of the magnetic core array. I will design this first because it will determine the overall layout for the system control board.

ৡৎ৯ঽ

Chapter 4 – Designing the Core Array

64 byte (8x8x8)

In the previous chapter we determined how to drive a single ferrite core so that we could set and retrieve flux states from that core. The next step is to figure out how to arrange a number of cores into an array such that we can store and retrieve actual data values which contain multiple bits.

For most designs we would have a target for the required number of bits in each data value and the number of these values which we need to store. The amount of data we need to store in our design is however totally arbitrary as we are only designing a demonstration system although it would be nice if the final design could be connected to a real computer system. With that in mind I decided that each data value would consist of 8 bits so that bytes of data could be stored and there will be a total of 64 bytes storage in the array. This results in the system requiring a modest 512 ferrite cores to give this storage capacity and while this is a very small number compared to a commercial system it is still sufficiently large that we need to give some careful though to the physical implementation.

We could simply pass all the X and Y conductors through each core in the same direction but this would make laying out the eight core mats difficult and also weaving the inhibit and sense wire would also be a problem. Because the sense output signal is so small we must try to minimise any possibility of the sense wire picking up external noise or cross talk from the other core wires so keeping these wires as short as possible is preferable.

As I have already mentioned we will be using a 3 wire design although we must provide the following four functions using just the three conductors which are passing through each core.

1) X selection partial current wire
2) Y selection partial current wire
3) Sense wire
4) Inhibit wire

The cores we will be using are very large compared to the cores which were in use for much of the life of magnetic core memory systems. They are however still very small as can be seen in figure 4-1 which shows a single core next to the tip of a ballpoint pen with a copper wire passed through the core. The copper wire is 0.05mm in diameter and there is a human hair alongside for comparison.

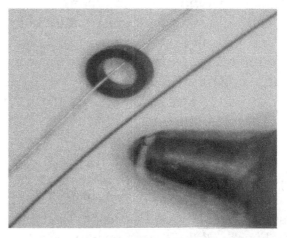

Figure 4-1 Ferrite Core size Comparison

Fortunately we do not have to have separate lines for every single core as they can easily be grouped into logical arrays.

When we address the memory we will need to supply it with a 6 bit address in order to select one of the 64 available bytes and selecting the required core will be taken care of by the decoder which we will design in a later chapter.

There are many different ways in which we could organise the individual cores to give us the required groups of bits but for this design I will be arranging them in 8 blocks with 64 cores in each block.

These blocks of cores will each be responsible for storing one of the bits in each byte and these blocks are normally referred to as 'mats' and so we will use that term from this point to refer to a set of cores which are used to store a particular bit in each byte value. For example all the cores in mat 3 will be responsible for storing bit 3 in all the byte addresses within our memory system.

We now need to figure out how to arrange the 64 cores which will form each mat and we can lay them out in a grid of 8x8 cores as shown in figure 4-2.

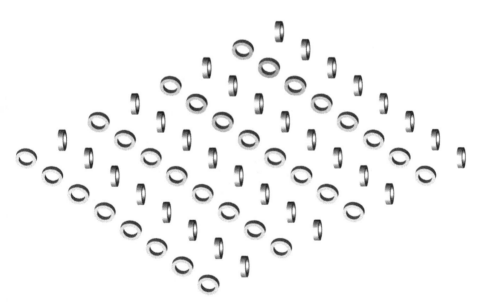

Figure 4-2 Ferrite Cores Orientation

Notice in this layout that the cores in each column are rotated by 90 degrees relative to the adjacent columns and I will explain the reason for this shortly.

The spacing of the core grid that we will be using is 2.5mm so that each row and column is spaced by 2.5mm.

Now that we have the cores laid out in a single mat we need to start by passing the coincidence selection wires through each core.

The cores will be addressed in 8 rows of 8 columns and so we can begin by passing the 'X' selection wires through each row of cores as shown in figure 4-3. Notice the arrows at the end of each wire which show the direction of current during a write of a '1' value to the cores. Each wire passes through all 8 cores in each row and so allows any one of the cores in each row to be selected by selecting the entire row but remember that this alone will not result in a strong enough magnetic field to cause the core flux to change state.

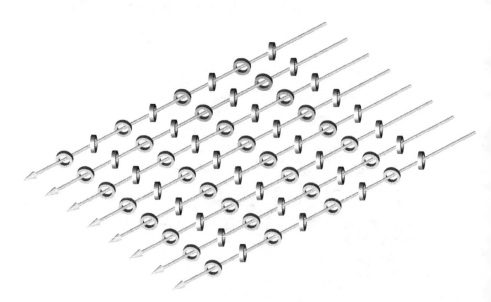

Figure 4-3 Core X selection wires

Next we pass the 'Y' selection wires through all the cores in each column of cores and this will allow us to select a column of cores but again remember that this alone will not result in a strong enough magnetic field to cause the core flux to change state.

However if we select both an 'X' wire and a 'Y' wire then the core where these two wires intersect will see a magnetic field from both wires and the total magnetic field for this core will then be sufficient to cause it to change state. All the other cores in this row and column will only see a single wire field and so no other cores will change state.

All the cores in the other rows and columns will not see any magnetic field at all as their wires do not have any current flowing in them and so they will also remain unchanged.

Because the cores in each column are rotated relative to the adjacent cores the required direction of the current in each column is also reversed. The reason for this arrangement will become clear shortly and figure 4-4 shows the arrangement of cores and X and Y wires. Note the current direction indication arrows at the end of each wire.

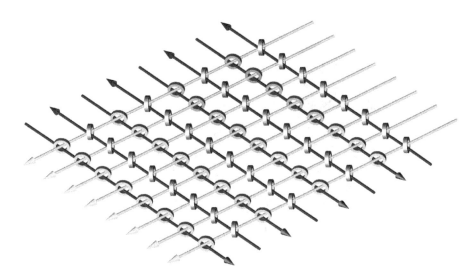

Figure 4-4 Core Y selection wires

Now that we have the core selection wires in place we need to add a sense wire to the cores so that we can detect any signals caused by a flux change in one of the cores. As the entire mat will only be used to store single bit in the byte value then only one core in each mat will ever be selected at one time and so we can use a single sense wire for every core in each mat and this wire will pass through all 64 cores in the mat. It is important that the sense wire passes through all the cores in the same direction relative the current flow direction in the selection wires. This is the reason that the cores in each column are rotated as it enables the sense wire to be more easily wound through all 64 cores without having too much excess wire. The only penalty for this is the need to drive each column current in opposite directions but we can easily arrange for that in our board track layout.

Figure 4-5 shows the addition of the sense wire and the purpose of alternating the direction of the 'Y' selection currents can now be more clearly understood as we can now see how reversing each column of cores makes weaving the sense wire much easier.

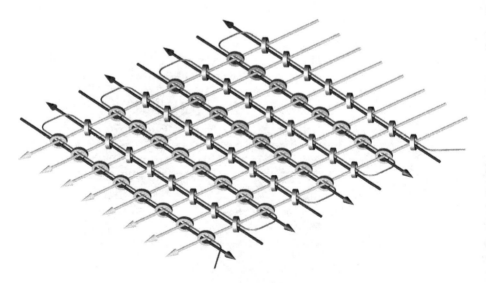

Figure 4-5 Sense wire added

The last wire we need to add is for the write inhibit line and this is wound in a similar way to the sense wire but starting at a different point. As with the sense wire the winding of this wire is made easier due to the alternating current direction in each 'Y' select wire. In commercial core memories there were many different approaches to the way in which the cores were physically constructed and they had to take other factors into account such as total core inductance, noise, capacitance are just a few of these but luckily we can almost ignore these issues because our core will be so small at just 512 cores.

Figure 4-6 shows the array with the inhibit wire added.

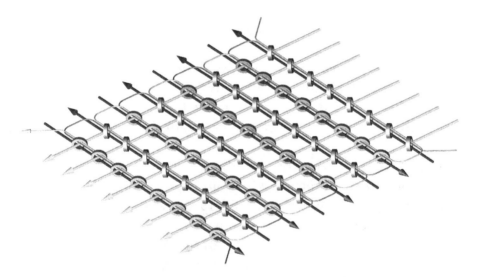

Figure 4-6 Inhibit Wire Added

Note that the current direction indicator is the current direction required to inhibit the writing of a '1'.

It may be difficult to see how the sense and inhibit wires are woven into the array so this is shown more clearly in figure 4-7.

Note that in the actual design I will be combining the sense and inhibit functions into a single wire but I am showing them as separate wires here to clarify the explanation.

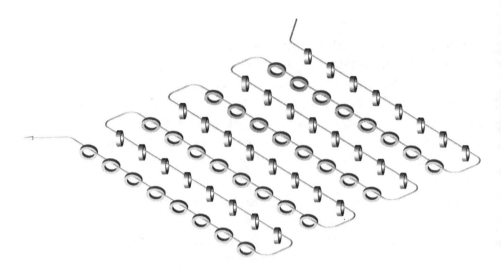

Figure 4-7 Sense and Inhibit wire detail

We now have the design for an individual mat but as I stated each mat will only be used to store an individual bit in the data byte. We therefore need another 7 mats to store the other 7 bits although most of the required wires are duplicates of those used in the first mat.

If we label the 8 'X' wires used in the first mat as X0 to X7 then we can extend these same 8 wires and pass them through the corresponding rows in each mat. Every 'X' wire will therefore pass through a total of 64 cores, 8 in each mat row.

We can do exactly the same thing with the 'Y' wires and so each 'Y' wire will also pass through 64 cores, 8 in each mat column.

This arrangement means that when we select an address we will always be selecting a set of 8 cores in the same location on each mat. For example if we set selection lines X3 and Y5 then we will be selecting the cores at location X3 and X5 in all 8 mats.

I should point out here that it does not actually matter if the core positions for each bit are the same in every mat. For example the bits for a particular memory address could be randomly scattered in each mat as long as the same cores are always selected for a specific memory address.

However it will make construction of the core array board much easier if all eight mats are laid out in a consistent manner.

The final choice we have to make is how to physically lay out the individual mats and again we have a number of choices.

When I was considering the layout I would use for this design I wanted to make sure that the final result was something that would be practical for others to construct. We have already seen that the cores are very small and having to string a large number of these onto very fine copper wires is always going to be a bit of a challenge but I decided on a design which would simplify the core assembly process as much as possible.

I also wanted a design in which the final result was visually interesting. After all it will take quite some effort to assemble one of these arrays and so it would be nice if the end result is something that looks as it should.

In addition I also wanted to separate the construction of the core array board from the electronics control and logic board. This was so that the overall boards could be smaller but also because the chances of damaging a core array which has taken many hours to assemble would be very high if it was part of the control board.

While it would have been easier to sub divide the overall core assembly into smaller individual boards with each of these boards hosting a single core mat I decided against this layout as it would require handling many more individual wires compared to the design I finally chose. I will describe this in more detail in a later chapter.

An added advantage of using a separate core array board is that it can be unplugged and individual cores can be connected to the control board sockets and this is very useful for test purposes.

Finally there was the cost to consider and as the control board was going to be a 4 layer board it was going to be far more cost effective to keep the dimensions of the control board as small as possible.

Many commercial core memory systems build each mat as one layer of a physical stack of cores such as is shown in figure 4-8.

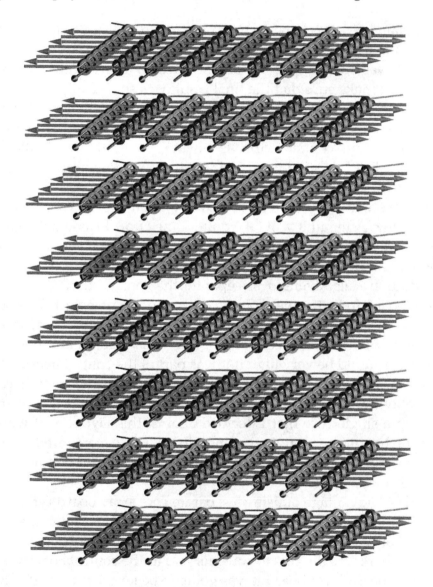

Figure 4-8 Stacked Core Array

However because our memory arrays are small we can lay them out on a single board to simplify construction as shown in figures 4-9 and 4-10.

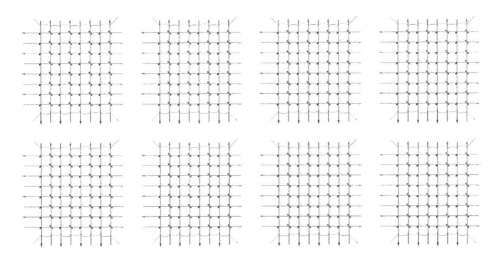

Figure 4-9 Simple Single Layer Core

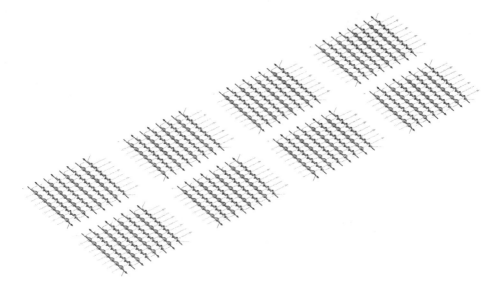

Figure 4-10 Single Layer Mat Perspective View

Each mat must have separate sense and inhibit function wires and so we will end up with the following wires in our full memory array.

1) 8x 'X' selection wires
2) 8x 'Y' selection wires
3) 8x sense wires (one for each mat)
4) 8x inhibit wires (one for each mat)

As I mentioned earlier our final design will actually use a combined sense and inhibit wire and so only 3 wires will pass through each core.

Figure 4-11 shows a close up photograph of a completed core mat and figure 4-12 shows a view of the entire memory core board.

The control circuitry is of course on the controller and interface board (shown later).

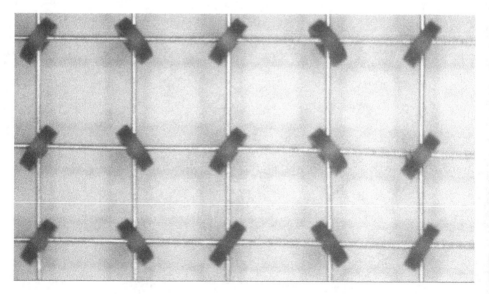

Figure 4-11 Close up of Part of Array Mat

Figure 4-12 Magnetic Core Array Board

The assembly of this core is somewhat tedious but is well within the capabilities of the average electronics enthusiast and I think you will agree that it closely resembles a commercial magnetic core memory system from 60 years ago although on a smaller scale.

The technology is certainly the same and as the purpose of this project is to develop a memory system using magnetic cores then we are well on our way to achieving that goal.

ৡ ৵ঙ

Chapter 5 – Designing the address decoder

At this point in our project we have determined how to use individual ferrite cores to store data and how to organise a number of cores into an array so that we can store this data in a structured way. We now need to design a circuit which will allow us to access each data byte within our memory system using an addressing scheme suitable for connection to a typical computer.

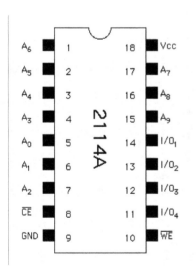

If we take a look at a simple static RAM chip pin out as depicted on the left then we can see the connections which are commonly implemented and also the standard designations given to these connections.

As our magnetic core memory system is intended to take the place of such a device then it is logical that we create an interface with compatible inputs and outputs as this will simplify its connection to a target machine.

I will briefly describe the purpose of each connection and how they will be used in our design.

The power connections (GND and Vcc) are of course used to provide a ground reference for all the input and output signals as well as supplying the device with power.

In our project we will need a 0V reference which we will refer to as GND and a single +5V supply which we will call VDD. Notice that the system will be designed to use a single supply rail which will greatly simplify it use.

In the device shown above the connections labelled A0 to A9 are the address selection inputs and we will use the same terminology although as our memory array is only 64 bytes in size we will only need 6 address lines in order to access it. We will therefore define them as A0 to A5.

I/O1 to I/O4 are the data input and out connections and because this is a 4 bit device it only uses 4 lines for this purpose. However our memory system will be 8 bit and so we will use 8 lines for this purpose. They will be defined as D0 to D7 and will serve as both data input and data output.

The _CE connection shown on the above device is the Chip Enable input and is used to enable the device output buffers so that it can drive its data lines on the bus it is connected to. This is an important feature of any memory device as it allows it to be connected to a shared data bus which is typically used in many computer systems. We will include a Chip Enable control input in our design and it will be defined as _CE and it will adhere to the most commonly used active low convention.

The _WE input is used to determine if data is to be read from the device or written to the device. When this input is high the device is in read (output) mode and when low it is in the write (input) mode.

In our system we will use a similar control input line and define it as RW such that we follow the same logic as described above.

I will identify the _WE control input as RW through the remainder of this book as this will make the explanations clearer.

All the other timing signals and control lines will be generated within our memory system to make it a self contained memory unit and as such it will not require further external timing signals.

The following table lists the inputs and outputs that we will include in our design.

Name	Direction	Purpose
D0	Input /output	Data byte 0
D1	Input /output	Data byte 1
D2	Input /output	Data byte 2
D3	Input /output	Data byte 3
D4	Input /output	Data byte 4
D5	Input /output	Data byte 5
D6	Input /output	Data byte 6
D7	Input /output	Data byte 7
A0	Input	Address byte 0
A1	Input	Address byte 1
A2	Input	Address byte 2
A3	Input	Address byte 3
A4	Input	Address byte 4
A5	Input	Address byte 5
_CE	Input	Chip enable (Active low)
RW	Input	Write enable (High = Read Low = Write)
GND	na	0V reference and power return
VDD	na	+5V power supply

Now that we have defined the various interface connections which we intend to use we must design a suitable control system that will take the signals indicated in the table above and use them to properly implement our memory system.

The first circuit we will look at is the address decoder as this is a very simple circuit to design. I will just clarify here that although it would be very much simpler to use something such as a microcontroller to control our memory system I do not feel that this would be in keeping with the stated goal of this book. I therefore intend to stick to TTL logic devices as this is much more in keeping with the type of technology we are developing and it should also make the project much more interesting.

Anyone wishing to develop their own magnetic core memory system could of course replace much of the control circuitry with a microcontroller or FPGA and create the required functionality in firmware in place of the hardware solution I will be presenting.

The first thing we will design is the actual address decoder as this is very easy to implement because all it needs to do is take a 6 bit address and select one of the 64 cores in each memory array mat. While this may sound complicated it is worth taking a moment to consider that it does not matter which core represents which data bit and so the decoder does not need to be configured to address the cores sequentially. It does not even matter if a different core is used in each mat for a specific data byte as long as the decoder is consistent in the way it selects the required cores. For example if we use the following terminology to identify individual cores.

X = the row on which the selected core is wired.
Y = the column on which the selected core is wired.
M = the mat into which the core is wired.

Then each individual core can be represented using something such as.
X3Y5M4
Which would represent the core in row 3 of column 5 on mat 4.

As stated above it does not matter what order the cores are used within a particular data byte and so, for example, the following cores could be used for a single data byte.

X3Y5M0 , X6Y2M1 , X4Y3M2 , X3Y2M3 , X2Y7M4 , X1Y0M5 , X2Y5M6 , X2Y5M7

As long as the decoder always selects these cores for a specific address then the system will work correctly. Note that although the last two cores are at the same X and Y locations they are on different mats and so we are referring to separate cores.

With that in mind we are free to organise our address decoder in whatever layout we prefer and we are not restricted to making each address use sequential cores in the memory array.

We now need to determine how we will take the 6 bit memory address and turn it into X and Y select values while making sure that only one X,Y combination is ever selected for each address.

As it turns out that is extremely easy to accomplish as all we need to do is use two 1 of 8 decoders such as the 74LS138.

Figure 5-1 shows how such a decoder arrangement can be constructed.

I will be presenting the actual schematics in later chapters but for now I will continue to use diagrams in order to keep the explanations as clear as possible.

As each system block is presented it is worth remembering that the techniques I am showing are only one possible way to achieve our design goal. The reader is encouraged to experiment with alternative methods and possibly improve on this system.

My main goal is to describe the way in which a magnetic core memory system fundamentally functions.

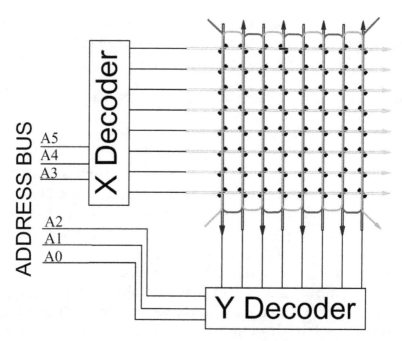

Figure 5-1 Single Mat X and Y selection decoder Concept

As we can see in Figure 5-1 any one of the 64 cores can be exclusively selected depending on the supplied 6 bit address value. Although I am only showing a single memory array mat in this diagram it should be noted that all the X row connections are connected to the same X decoder outputs and all the Y column connections are connected to the same Y decoder outputs. This arrangement means that 8 cores are selected, one from each mat, for each possible address.

I will now need to represent all the memory array mats in the following diagrams and so the diagrams will not show individual cores but rather the entire array of mats as depicted in figure 5-2.

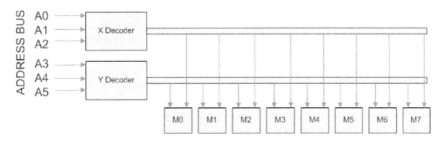

Figure 5-2 Array X and Y selection decoder Concept

In figure 5-2 each block labelled M0 to M7 represents one of the 64 ferrite core arrays and as we can see they are all wired in parallel.

Now that we can select any set of 8 memory cores by simply supplying a 6 bit address the next step is to arrange our inhibit connections. If you recall there is only one inhibit line for each memory mat and so we will end up with a total of 8 inhibit lines as shown in figure 5-3. For clarity we will show the 8 inhibit lines as a bus comprising of one inhibit line for each of the 8 mats.

The inhibit lines are controlled by a set of drivers through the inhibit control logic circuits which are in turn supplied with the data we wish to write into the memory array.

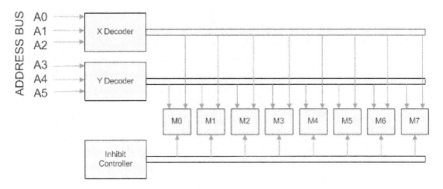

Figure 5-3 Inhibit Control Concept

Next we need to add the sense lines to our diagram and although the core mats are still shown as single blocks remember that this will represent 64 cores in each mat and the eight mats form our entire 512 core memory array structure.

As can be seen in figure 5-4 we have a total of 32 lines running through the memory core although we do of course also have connections to both ends of these wires which we will look at in more detail later. I will also mention here that the system will combine the inhibit and sense functions into a single wire so only 24 wires will be present in the final design.

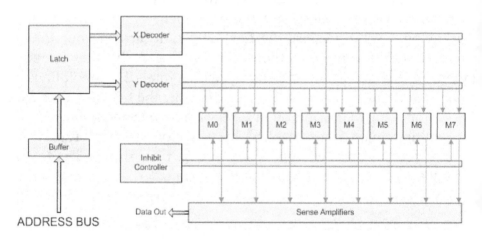

Figure 5-4 Core Arrangement Simplified concept

For now we can see that we have our memory core connections arranged in such a way that we can develop the overall design of our core memory system and the next step is to determine how data will move in and out of the memory cores.

I have added a few additional features to the diagram in figure 5-4 including an address buffer with a latch although these are shown in a simplified arrangement. I will describe these in more detail as we progress through the development of our memory system but I will outline their purpose very briefly here.

There are a few complications with interfacing a core memory compared to a static RAM chip and we need to deal with those if our system is to work properly.

To begin with we should buffer all incoming connections and so I have added a buffer to the address bus and also a latch which will be used to store the current address which has been selected. Hopefully the reasons for doing this will become clear as the circuits take shape.

I have shown the inhibit line driver and also the sense amplifiers although they are simply represented as logical elements in this diagram. We will design suitable circuits in a later chapter.

At the top right of the diagram I have also shown two current source blocks, One for the Y lines and one for the X lines. Although there are eight of each type of line we only need two line driver current sources because only one X and one Y line will ever be active at the same time.

Before we proceed with the conceptual design phase we need to consider some specifics in designing a magnetic core memory. In particular we need to remember that when we perform a read of the memory core this action effectively erases the data from the cores which have just been read and so we need to include a mechanism which is able to restore the data back to its value prior to the read. It should be noted here that most commercial core memory systems included a feature which allowed the writing back of the erased data to be skipped as it was not always needed and by skipping this step the performance of the memory system could be increased.

For example if a memory location was going to be read and then immediately updated there was no value in writing the original value back into the memory so this step could be skipped and the new data value written to the memory location instead.

To keep our initial development as simple as possible I will not be including this feature in the first version of our system but as it is a feature of the control logic we can always add it later should we want to with possibly an additional data buffer.

Having considered the requirements then our next addition to the design is a data input buffer at the system interface and as with the address buffer the incoming data will be stored in a latch.

There are a number of reasons for using latches to store the address and data values but primarily they are used to eliminate the need for critical timing with the host processor. Once we have read and latched the address and data values the address and data busses can be released but the address and data values will be retained.

We should note here that the data bus which is used for incoming data is only used in memory write mode and not in memory read mode.

In addition to storing the incoming data byte the system will also need to store the data value it reads from the memory core in another data register. The reason it needs to store the data read from the core in a separate register is because as previously noted the action of reading the data causes the data to be deleted from the selected memory location. By storing the data value which has been read in a register we have the ability to write it back into the core once the read has been completed.

This brings us on to another element we need to add to the circuit and this is a means by which we can select which data byte to write into the memory core.

Write Mode Phase

In write mode all we will need to do is store the data value which has been latched into the incoming data register into memory at the currently selected address after first erasing the existing data by performing a dummy read.

Read Mode Phase

Read mode is similar to write mode but it will require us to restore the data value we read from the memory at the current address back into the memory at the same address. The read cycle begins by reading the data value from memory into the memory data buffer and this action deletes the stored data but the data value that was stored is now in the buffer. We then write the value stored in the buffer register back into the memory and finally we put the data onto the data bus so that it is available to the host processor.

In order that we can select which data byte value we wish to write into the memory we must add a multiplexer which selects either of the two data bytes. Figure 5-5 shows the conceptual system with these additional features added.

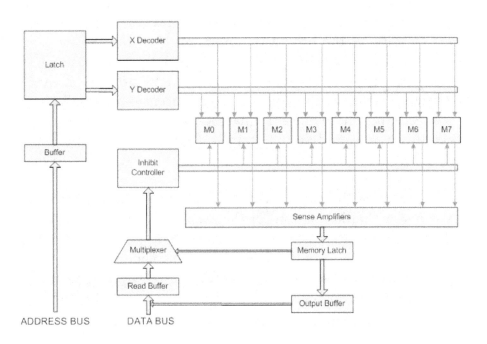

Figure 5-5 Conceptual Memory System Data Flow

Finally we will need to add some sort of logic control to our memory system so that we can create the required sequences of operations which will be needed in order to make our core memory system functional.

This logic control will be responsible for writing data into the memory core and also providing the multi-step sequence which is required for the data read and write operations.

When I initially started thinking about this project I was intending to add additional control and status lines to the memory system but I wanted it to behave more like a more modern static RAM memory device. In almost all systems which implemented a magnetic core memory system as the data storage mechanism a series of timing and control signals were added to make the memory operate quickly and efficiently with the host system. The required timing sequence required to make a magnetic core memory system function correctly and reliably is very complex and is also critical in terms of some of the timing requirements. I wanted to avoid the need to build a custom processor system to make use of our memory design and so took the decision to produce a system architecture which eliminated the need for custom control signals and so act much more like a normal SRAM.

While this may sound simple it adds significant complexity to the design but has the benefit of not needing modifications to every system it is connected to.

Figure 5-6 shows the design with our logic control added and again this is just a simple diagram of the system. We will begin to add detail to each functional block in later chapters.

I have purposefully kept the diagrams and explanations as simple as possible but even so you can probably already appreciate that a magnetic core memory system is a relatively complex thing to design.

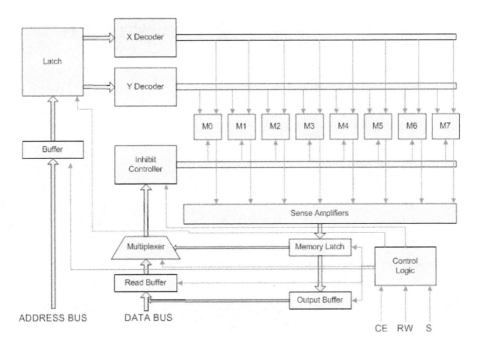

Figure 5-6 Adding Control Logic

Control Logic Features

The control logic circuit will be responsible for controlling all the operations within the memory system including the following.

1) Write / Erase cycle
2) Read / write back cycle
3) Core write timing through strobe of the A,Y select lines
4) Read sense amplifier strobe
5) Latching incoming data
6) Latching the supplied memory address
7) Putting the read data value into the data bus
8) Strobe the inhibit lines
9) Triggering a write or read cycle
10) Power up inhibit hold off

I will describe most of these functions along with their associated circuit designs in dedicated chapters although inevitably some of them are interdependent.

One point to bear in mind is that there are any number of ways in which a magnetic core memory system can be designed and in this book I am hoping to generate interest in this technology so you should feel free to design your own version of the system.

An interesting feature of this type of system is that it encompasses many different elements of electronics and mechanical design so is a fascinating subject and one which I hope you will continue to research when you finish this book, but hopefully not before.

Designing a system such as this is a fascinating challenge because it requires electronic circuits to be designed which are capable of driving high speed current pulses into highly inductive loads while at the same time being able to reliably detect multiple small level signals. The output signals from the core memory are in the order of just a few tens of millivolts but the currents required to drive the core wires is in the hundreds of milliamps range. The sense wire output signals are also very rapid and timing critical.

In addition to these challenges we must also design the control logic which needs to accurately time and control the core drive and sense circuits for a large number of driver circuits.

All of these challenges will make this development task a very interesting to anyone looking for a challenging and unusual project.

ℰℒℋℰ

Chapter 6 – Memory Cycle Trigger

In the previous chapter I listed a number of actions that the system control logic would need to be responsible for.

---

1) Write cycle
2) Read / write back cycle
3) Core write timing through strobe of the A,Y select lines
4) Read sense amplifier strobe
5) Latching incoming data
6) Latching the supplied memory address
7) Putting the read data value into the data bus
8) Strobe the inhibit lines
9) Triggering a write or read cycle
10) Power up inhibit hold off

Each of these will require the design of not only the logic control circuits but also the circuits which will carry out the actual memory core drive functions. Because the circuits which will carry out these operations are dependant to a very large degree on the control logic I have decided to include both the logic design and system circuits together in each chapter instead of what may be viewed as a more traditional approach of describing them separately. Hopefully this approach will help in making the explanations and circuit operation easier to follow.

A magnetic core memory system is a collection of highly interdependent sub systems and so is difficult to describe in a sequential manner but I will try to make the operation as clear as possible.

I will be starting with item number 9 in the above list as this is not really part of the magnetic core memory system but is a feature I decided to add in order to make the system behave more like a static RAM device.

The action of reading data into or out of a magnetic core memory actually requires a number of carefully timed steps and we will need to design circuits which will carry out these steps. However I wanted our system to function without the need for specific external signals which magnetic core memory systems normally require.

One of these is a signal to instruct the memory to begin a cycle such as a read or a write. If we are to have the system operate in the same way as an SRAM device then the only signals we will be providing are the _CE and RW inputs. Unfortunately these are not really sufficient because although we could, for example, use the _CE line to trigger the memory operation we would need the host processor to toggle that line every time it wanted to read a different memory address and that is not the way an SRAM would normally operate.

Fortunately we can fairly easily create a circuit to give us the required functionality and generate a memory trigger signal without the need for special actions by the host system.

From the control logic perspective we want the memory to be updated every time we change the address so that the data at the newly selected address is presented on the data output.

We also want the memory to perform a read or write cycle if we enable the device or switch from a read to a write mode.

I therefore designed a circuit to provide a 'START' pulse whenever any of the inputs indicated above changed state.

Figure 6-1 shows the circuit which will perform this function.

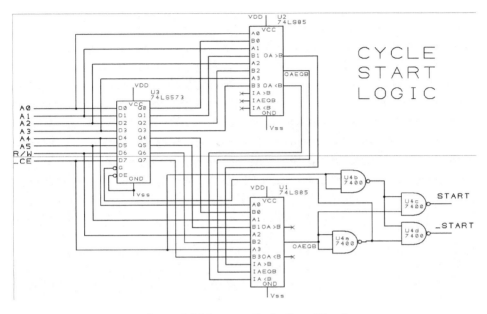

Figure 6-1 Memory Cycle Start Circuit

It may seem odd starting with a part of the design which I am stating is not really part of the system but as this circuit will be responsible for triggering the memory read or memory write process then by getting this circuit working first we have a good starting point for the rest of the system.

This circuit also provides the additional function of latching the supplied memory address and so starting here will simplify the rest of the development process.

In the diagram I showed in the previous chapter we included a latch so that we could capture the address which was present at the start of the memory cycle but I added this latch for a secondary function which I will now describe.

If we examine the circuit in figure 6-1 we can see that the latch (U3) is connected to address lines A0 to A5 on the address bus but we can also see that it is connected to the chip enable (_CE) and read, write (RW) lines.

When we strobe the latch enable input of this latch (LE) the current status levels of the 6 address lines along with the _CE and RW will be stored in the latch.

We therefore have buffered and stored the currently requested memory address but you will notice that the 8 lines are also connected to an 8 bit magnitude comparator comprising of IC U1 and IC U2. This magnitude comparator monitors the input and output of the latch and if the output does not match the input it will lower the equals (=) output which is passed through an inverter to the latch enable input of the latch. The operation of this circuit is very simple as it just generates a short pulse whenever the address or one of the two control lines is changed.

This pulse is used to update the latch but it is also used as the start signal for the memory read or memory write process. As this signal is generated automatically whenever one of the 8 input lines changes it eliminates the need for a separate memory strobe line.

The reason for including the chip enable line is to force the memory system to perform either a read or write of the current address if the chip enable line is asserted.

The memory process is also automatically started if the supplied memory address is changed and so the host processor can perform sequential memory access, read or write, without having to toggle the chip enable line.

By including the write enable line we can also force the memory system to start the memory cycle by simply changing the state of this line without altering either the chip enable or memory address. This allows the host system to perform a memory write followed by a read or vice versa without having to toggle any other lines.

To avoid unwanted memory cycles I have included a couple of gates in IC U4 which allow the start signal to be blocked when the chip enable line is high.

This circuit can be further improved by adding a cycle state gating feature to prevent erratic operation if the control lines are changed during a memory read or write cycle but I will leave that for the reader to implement should they wish.

We now have a start and inverted start signal which we can use in the following chapters to develop the magnetic core memory control logic circuits.

If you prefer you could of course omit this trigger circuit entirely and use an explicit memory request input but this is up to you and how you intend to use the memory system. If you do decide to do away with the trigger circuit you should add a latch and suitable control logic to store the supplied memory address for reasons which I will explain later.

The final design of this system includes a number of jumpers to allow the user to select either automatic start operation or an external start pulse along with selection of either gated or non gated start pulse control.

ຂໆຮ

Chapter 7 – Read Sense Amplifier

In chapter 3 we investigated the characteristics of the ferrite core which we will be using for this magnetic core memory project and as a result of the tests we were able to determine the signals we can expect from the memory core sense wires. These signals are how we determine the data values which are stored in the memory cores.

The sense output signals are however very low in amplitude at just a few tens of thousandths of a volt (mV) and have very specific timing relative to the core selection pulses. We must therefore design a circuit which is capable of detecting these pulses and storing the intended data bit values in a digital buffer.

I am attempting to keep the overall design of this system as simple as possible and part of that requirement is to minimise the number of power supply rails that will be needed. In commercial magnetic core memory systems there are normally several power rails required because of the need to drive large and highly inductive core arrays. However we have the advantage that our memory core will only contain 512 cores in total and this means that we should be able to simplify some of the required drive circuits as the expected loads will be a little less complex.

The read sense amplifier is one such circuit and we can greatly simplify the design of this in two ways. If we design the sense amplifier and inhibit drive circuits to work in harmony with each other then our design task will be much easier.

To achieve this I decided to connect one end of the sense and inhibit wire to 0V. The reason for this will become apparent later.

In this chapter we can focus on designing a single power rail sense amplifier which only needs to detect the read pulses which are generated in the sense wire during the memory read sequence.

If we take another look at the signal we are trying to detect then we can begin putting together a suitable amplifier circuit.

If you recall from chapter 3 then the pulse in the sense wire can be either positive or negative depending on the polarity of the magnetic core magnetisation switch. While it does not make any real technical difference which polarity of signal we use I decided to use the positive going signal pulse to indicate that a one (1) was stored in the memory ferrite core.

Figure 7-1 shows the signal we can expect from the sense line and it also shows the relative timing of the selection current pulse.

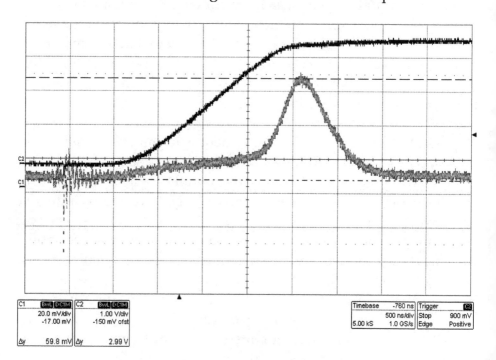

Figure 7-1 Magnetisation switch Output Signal

The amplitude of the pulse we are trying to detect is approximately 60mV peak and occurs around 2uS after the start of the rising edge of the selection current pulse.

Note that in the actual complete array the sense output signal is very much smaller than is shown here and I will get back to the reasons for that in a later chapter.

For now I will use the current test set up as it will help to make the explanations clear.

The circuit we need to design in this chapter must take a timing pulse which is 2.0uS in duration and on the rising edge it will trigger the selection current drivers and on the falling edge it will latch the output from the sense amplifier into a memory read buffer.

By combining these control operations into a single circuit we can greatly simplify the control logic which will be required to drive our memory system.

When contemplating the best approach for the design of the sense amplifier I considered using a differential amplifier and buffer package such as those used in the original commercial magnetic memory systems. Unfortunately these devices are hard to find and are therefore very expensive and as I wanted any parts to be readily available then I had to exclude them from the design. They are also not really needed in a system such as the one we are designing here as you will shortly see. I next considered using a single supply operational amplifier but this was not really in keeping with the design goals and so again I discounted them as a possibility.

Having spent some time considering the options I decided that the best approach would be a very simple circuit that made direct use of the type of signal we are trying to detect. That signal is really a current induced in the sense wire and so it would be simple to use the sense wire as an element in a simple amplifier circuit which used a transistor as the amplifier.

Because the sense signal is of such low amplitude it cannot be used to directly drive a transistor as the signal level would never get high enough to turn on a transistor junction.

I could of course have created a balanced voltage divider but because of the nature of the memory core array it would have been very difficult to make it work reliably and so I selected a more direct approach and the resulting circuit is shown in Figure 7-2.

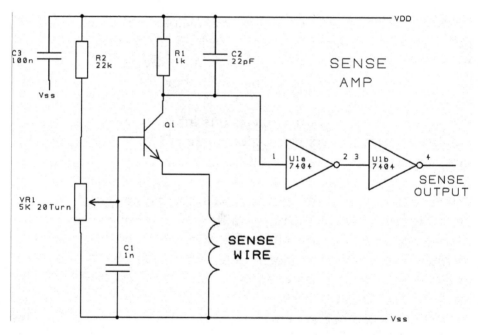

Figure 7-2 Sense Amplifier Circuit

In this circuit the sense wire is placed in the emitter ground path of a single transistor amplifier stage and the transistor base response is controlled by a simple resistor voltage divider and damping capacitor. For better noise immunity the 7404 could be replaced by a 7414 which has much better noise rejection capability.

The action of this circuit is very simple and is largely self correcting as long as suitable value resistors are selected. As the short duration current pulse in the sense wire increases it has a tendency to increase the transistor emitter voltage but capacitor C2 connected to the base of the transistor prevents the base voltage from rising and so the transistor is forced to turn off until C2 has charged. This causes the collector voltage to rise and trigger the TTL inverter gate and as a result a squared up digital signal is produced whenever a positive going core switching current is detected. This signal represents a binary value of one (1) from the sense wire and can be used directly by a suitable latch to store the data value. When a negative going pulse is present on the sense wire the sense amplifier simply ignores it and no output pulse is produced. This simple circuit therefore provides the exact functionality that is required and with the simple addition of a latch we have the memory sense amplifier and read buffer completed.

The next step is to determine how and when to latch the data which the sense amplifier has read from the memory core.

To determine this I connected the sense amplifier to the core test setup which I described in chapter 3 and this allowed me to properly test its performance and response.

It must be noted here that the actual tests I carried out were more complex than I am indicating here because the circuits I am developing would be connected to a complete memory array consisting of 512 cores.

Each wire in the core actually passes through 64 cores and not just one as I am demonstrating at the moment and all of the wires are cross coupled to other wires with multiple cores because of the way in which the wires are woven through the cores.

However the generally design concepts I am describing are still valid and simply need careful circuit design in order that they function correctly in the full system.

I will come back to this aspect of the design later.

Figure 7-3 shows the amplifier response when no sense wire signal is present.

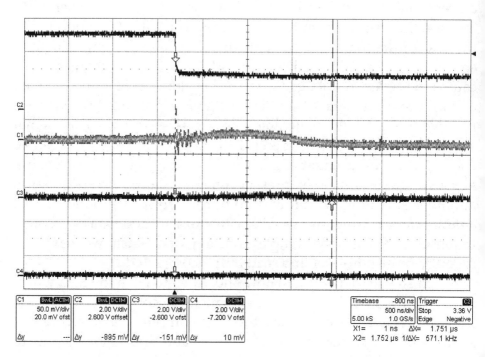

Figure 7-3 Sense Output with no Magnetisation Switch

In this diagram the top trace is the drive for the selection current pulse and the falling edge is therefore the timing reference.

The second trace down is the output of the sense wire and as can be seen there is no signal present.

The third trace down is the analogue output from the sense amplifier and the bottom trace is the output from the second inverter and again no signal is present so this would represent a zero (0) value read from the core.

Figure 7-4 shows the same four signals but when a positive going signal pulse is present on the sense wire.

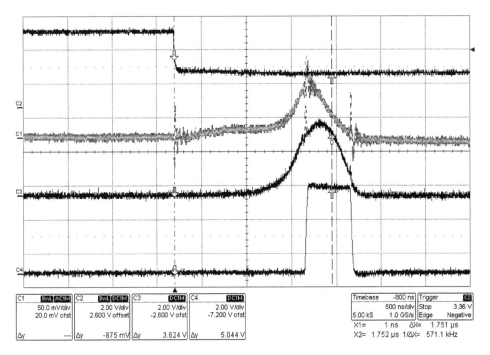

Figure 7-4 Sense Output with Magnetisation Switch

As can be seen the output from the sense wire is a pulse which is generated when the core flips magnetisation state and has an amplitude of approximately 60mV.

The analogue output from the sense amplifier is a positive pulse of around 4.5V peak amplitude and this triggers the TTL inverters which provide a nicely squared up digital output which is shown in the bottom trace.

The diagram also shows vertical cursor lines which have been aligned with the falling edge of the selection pulse and the centre of the TTL output pulse. The time between these two cursor lines is 1.75uS and this therefore gives us the required timing for the latching of the data read from the memory core by the sense amplifiers.

All that is required is to latch the data present in the output of these circuits 1.75uS after the selection pulse leading edge and we will be able to reliably save the data into the memory read buffer latch.

Figure 7-5 shows the response of the circuit when the output from the sense wire is negative going as it would be when the memory cores are written although we would not be interested in the output of the sense wire at that time and so no pulse is required.

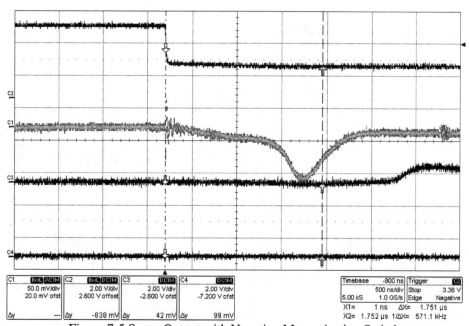

Figure 7-5 Sense Output with Negative Magnetisation Switch

As we can see there is no output from the sense amplifier when the memory core is either already in the zero (0) state or when the memory cores are written to and this is exactly what we need.

A very simple circuit but it performs the function we need it to.

As I stated earlier the actual sense wire signals levels in the final design will be very much lower in amplitude than is shown in these diagrams and are closer to 20mV but the circuit is the same.

We will now add the circuit required to correctly transfer the data from the sense amplifier into the memory read latch.

As ever there are many ways we could achieve this but as we will need the data from the sense amplifier to both restore the data into the memory cores and make this data available to the host processor bus then the easiest method is to use a latch.

The output of this latch can then be passed to a multiplexer so that it can be used by the other circuits in our system.

In general there are two types of latch available which would meet our needs but they differ in an important way.

The first type of latch is referred to as a transparent latch because when the latch enable pin is asserted the data on the input is transferred into the latch and the data stored in the latch will continue to change if the data on the input pin changes. This will continue until the latch enable pin is de-asserted. If the output of such a latch is also enabled then as long as the latch enable input is active the data output pins will immediately reflect any changes on the input pins, hence the term 'transparent latch'.

This is not really suitable for our application because the data on the input pins of the latch which is from the sense amplifier is only present for a short amount of time as we have seen earlier in this chapter and so the second type of latch would be much better for this application.

This type of latch is called an edge triggered latch because the data on the input pins is transferred into the latch during a transition of the latch enable pin. Once the latch enable edge has passed then the data on the input pins can change but the data stored in the latch will not be altered.

This will work better for us as it means that as long as the latch enable edge occurs at the correct time in the memory read cycle then the data from the sense amplifiers will be correctly stored in the latch. As we saw in figure 7-4 this latch enable edge needs to occur during the time when the data output from the sense amplifier buffers is available.

This window is between 1.50-2.0uS and so if we aim for 1.75uS we should have a good margin of error to ensure that the data is captured in a consistent and reliable way.

Figure 7-6 shows the circuit with the latch timing and latch added.

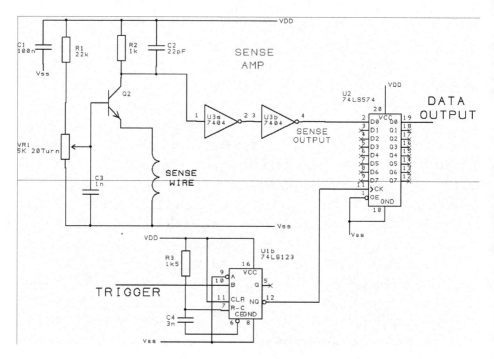

Figure 7-6 Sense Amp with Trigger and Latch

In this circuit we now have a pulse timer formed by U1b which is a 74ls123 with the capacitor and resistor values selected to provide a delay of 1.75uS.

The trigger input is derived from the selection line current pulse control circuit and the output of U1b is used to latch the data from the sense amplifier output into the latch which is a 74ls574 edge triggered octal latch.

This schematic only shows a single sense amplifier but there are of course 8 of these, one for each of the memory array mats. The data from the other 7 sense amplifiers can be fed into this same latch to give us the full 8 bit data value.

Because the trigger pulse is derived from the core selection line current pulse circuit we can be sure that the timing of the latch relative to the sense amplifier outputs will be correct.

Figure 7-7 shows the signals obtained from this circuit and as we can see the timing of the data latch is correct.

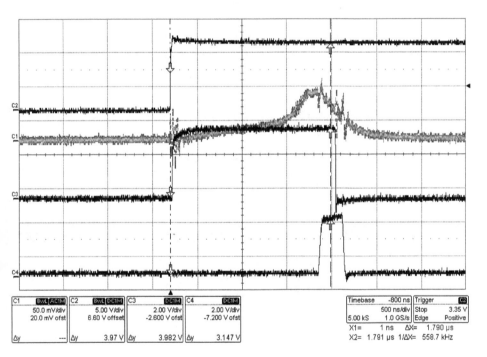

Figure 7-7 Sense Latch Control Signals

In this diagram the bottom trace is the data output from the sense amplifier buffer and the top trace is the trigger signal from the selection line pulse control circuit.

The second trace from the bottom is the output from the timing pulse generator (U1 in figure 7-6) and as we can see this is triggered by the rising edge of the current pulse control signal and the falling edge occurs near the centre of the data valid period of the sense amplifier output.

The timing between these two events is 1.75uS and figure 7-8 shows the output of the latch when a data value of one (1) is present on the sense amplifier output at the time of the latch falling edge.

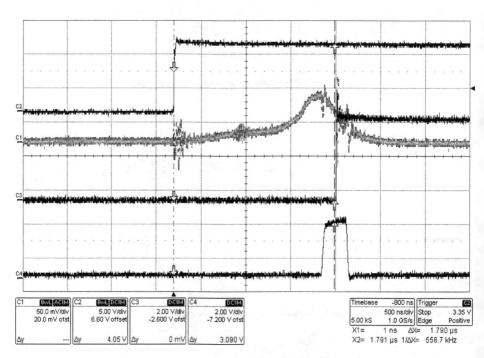

Figure 7-8 Sense Latch Output

In figure 7-8 the second trace up now shows the output from the data latch while the bottom trace shows the output from the sense amplifier. It is clear that the data value from the sense amplifier which was high at the time of the latch falling edge has been successfully stored in the latch. Had the data value from the sense amplifier been low during the latch period then the output from the latch would of course be low.

So although we now have a working memory read sense amplifier and latch circuit there is still a problem with it which we should address here. If we look at the signals in figure 7-8 it can be seen that the time required between the start of the selection pulse and the completion of latching the data into the buffer is around 2uS and this is a little on the slow side. It does not really matter as this system is only intended to be experimental but I though I would demonstrate how we can increase the performance of our system.

Further development to improve the performance still further would also be a very interesting project once the initial system development has been completed. It should however be noted that magnetic core memory systems operate in a very time dependant manner and so any modifications must be made with the overall operation of the system in mind.

The major limiting factor in the current speed of operation is the slow rise time of the selection pulse current which you may recall I intentionally slowed down in order to reduce the directly coupled current which was induced in the sense wire with a rapidly rising edge. The changes I made almost entirely eliminated this induced current spike as can be seen in figure 7-3 but we do not need to totally eliminate it as long as we set up the sense amplifier accordingly. The component values which I have selected for the sense amplifier shown in figure 7-2 actually allow for a larger amplitude secondary current spike and so we can adjust the selection current rising edge rate to shorten the overall memory read cycle time without needing to modify the sense amplifier.

Figure 7-9 shows the output signal from the sense wire when the rising edge of the selection current pulse is reduced from 2uS to 1uS and as can be seen the amplitude of the induced secondary current in the sense wire is much larger then it was in figure 7-3.

The amplitude has risen from around 5mV to almost 15mV but this signal level is still well below the switching threshold of the sense amplifier and so does not create any false memory reads.

In fact the faster rising current pulse actually increases the amplitude of the valid data read signal in the sense wire as can be seen in figure 7-10.

Note that the point at which the data must now be latched into the buffer has also moved and is now 850nS from the falling edge of the current selection pulse compared to the original 1.79uS shown in figure 7-8.

The latch timing can be adjusted using the variable resistor in the pulse time circuit which is shown in figure 7-6.

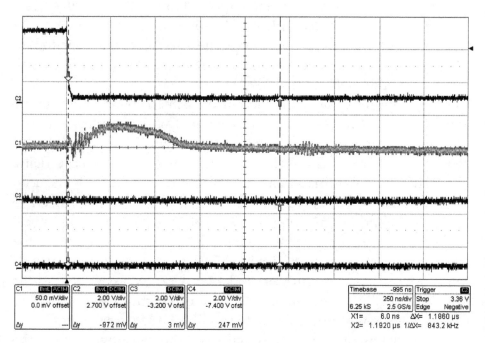

Figure 7-9 Coupled Output with faster Rising Edge

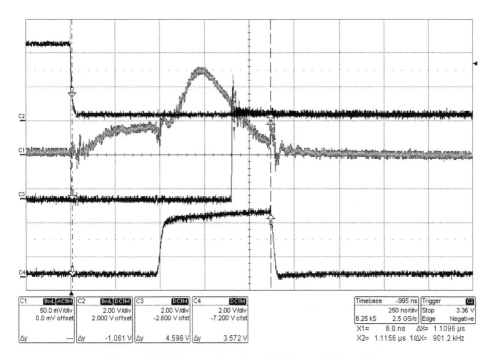

C1	BwL ACTM	C2	BwL DC1M	C3	DC1M	C4	DC1M		Timebase	-995 ns	Trigger	C2
	50.0 mV/div		2.00 V/div		2.00 V/div		2.00 V/div			250 ns/div	Stop	3.36 V
	0.0 mV offset		2.000 V offset		-2.600 V ofst		-7.200 V ofst		6.25 kS	2.5 GS/s	Edge	Negative
									X1=	6.0 ns	ΔX= 1.1096 µs	
Δy	---	Δy	-1.061 V	Δy	4.596 V	Δy	3.572 V		X2=	1.1156 µs	1/ΔX= 901.2 kHz	

Figure 7-10 Output Signals with Faster Rising Edge

A further advantage of the shorter time delay between the start of selection pulse and the latch time is that the likely error in this timing is now much smaller. Note that in figures 7-9 and 7-10 the time base has been changed to 250nS per division compared to 500nS per division in the earlier traces. Because the time delay is now shorter but the signal pulse width in the sense wire is approximately the same then any error in the width of the latch pulse delay is less likely to result in timing problems.

These modifications result in a memory read cycle time being reduced from over 2.0uS to around 1.0uS and so memory operational speed is doubled.

In figure 7-10 we can see that after adjusting the latch pulse timing we can still successfully read data values from the memory core and store them in the buffer latch.

As I progressed through the development of this magnetic core memory system I spent a great deal of time testing and optimising the various circuits with the aim of producing a system which could be considered practical.

The versions of the schematics shown in the remainder of this book will be for the final version of the system design which has significantly better performance than the initial test configuration.

For example the latch pulse time which was initially 1.75uS was reduced to just 400nS and this represents the read access time for the memory system.

This compares very favourably to magnetic core memory systems designed back in the 1950's and 1960's.

In order to achieve much faster operation speed for the system I used a different method to discriminate between the direct coupled signals and the sense pulse output.

Instead of using a current rate control I actually did the opposite and increased the switching speed of the wire driver circuits. The design changes reduced the switch on time for the drivers from 1.80uS to just 25nS. This did of course result in very large direct coupled signals being produced in the sense wires but the sense amplifier and latch timing was designed to selectively ignore the large direct coupled signals and operate the latch based on the much smaller signals produced by the core flux transitions.

To give you some idea how well this simple circuit works it is worth bearing in mind that the direct coupled signals produce pulses in the sense wire with an amplitude of around 2000mV while the signals produced by the flux transitions are a mere 20mV and occur approximately 80nS after the direct coupled pulse.

To further complicate the design task it should also be considered that the cores do not all produce exactly the same responses when they change flux state and of course there are also 64 cores on each sense wire and not just one as we have looked at so far.

Although the output enable pin on the latch is shown in the diagram as being tie to ground which permanently enables the latch output we could of course use this to control the data output from the latch should we need this later.

We now have the required circuit for reading data from the memory core and saving this data into a latch which was the stated goal for this chapter.

We still have some way to go before the memory system could be considered to be functional because as I already stated the process of reading the data from the memory cores erases them so we must find a way to deal with that and also add a number of other required features which I will explain as we progress.

ৡৎৡঔ

Chapter 8 – Current Source Pulse Generator

In this chapter we will design a suitable current controlled pulse generator circuit for our core memory system.

In the tests I have been describing so far the pulses applied to the ferrite core have been generated using a signal generator and a few driver transistors. To reverse the current flow I used a switch fitted between the core wire and the pulse source.

We now need to design a circuit which allows these actions to be performed under control of the logic circuits which we are designing and by designing the pulse generator we will know exactly what is required from the control circuits in order to properly drive it.

The pulse circuit will need to provide the following functions:

1) Accurate current pulse width generation
2) Current amplitude control
3) Current direction control for read and write operations

A limiting factor which we must consider is the use of a single power supply because this will have a major influence on the type of circuit we can use in this design.

We also need to consider that the system needs to generate relatively high current pulses but only in 2 wires at the same time as only a single X and a single Y wire will ever be active together.

There are actually up to 10 wires requiring current pulse control if we include the inhibit lines but I will only concentrate on the X and Y selection pulses in this chapter and we can take a look at designing the inhibit line driver circuit in the next chapter.

The required current in the selection wires is 350mA as we determined in an earlier chapter and so we will need to use switching devices that can reliably handle that current. Luckily there are quite a few such devices to choose from but as already indicated I wanted to keep the nature of the design as period appropriate as possible and so I decided to only consider bipolar transistors for this application.

Because we will need the circuit to provide both read and write current pulses it must be able to produce current in either polarity in the wires and so we will need to ensure that it can reliably generate short duration pulses with controlled current rise times in either direction into a load that will consist of a very low resistance but highly inductive load.

Anyone familiar with bipolar transistors will immediately recognise a potential difficulty here which is the need to drive then relatively hard in order to minimise the switching times. Unfortunately this generally requires that the transistors are driven into saturation but once a bipolar transistor has been driven into saturation it can take several micro seconds for the transistor to turn back off. Because of the requirements in the design of our magnetic core memory system we cannot afford to wait several micro seconds for the devices to turn back off once a current has been applied to a wire and so the circuits will need to be very carefully designed to ensure very fast switching speed in both the switch on and the switch off phase of operation.

From a design perspective none of these requirements are difficult to achieve if we design a full control circuit with all these factors taken into account. This type of circuit generally requires some fairly complex electronics in order to meet the requirements I have just outlined.

However I needed to be mindful that the system we are designing would require 24 of these circuits in total and so I needed to create a circuit to meet our requirements but which used a minimal number of components.

The required drive currents are also relatively high and beyond the capability of most small signal transistors although using large power devices was not really a practical solution due to both cost and size limitations.

A further restriction which I have already mentioned is my decision to use a single 5 volt power supply rather than a more usual multi rail system. While this will make the final memory system far more practical to use with small microprocessor systems it does make driving something like a core memory array much more difficult.

Luckily there are a number of suitable devices available to us and so I put together a circuit which not only meets our design goal but is also very cost effective to implement. It also meets other design requirements which I will come back to in later chapters.

The basic wire driver circuit is shown in figure 8-1.

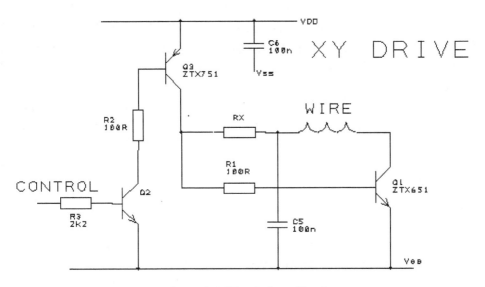

Figure 8-1 Wire Driver Circuit

With the basic specification in mind I started by designing a simple current switching circuit which would be suitable for use in a bridge circuit so that it could generate bidirectional current pulses.

Its operation is very simple and makes use of a high and low switching transistor which we will need in the final bridge circuit.

The component count is kept low by having the high switching transistor control the lower transistor and by incorporating an LCR filter made up of C5, RX and the core wire to control the current switching rate. In order to keep the memory cycle time as short as possible the pulse rise time is only slowed during the read phase.

Resistor RX is selected to provide the required selection pulse current and the value of C5 provides the current rate and hence the switching time of the circuit which must of course be controlled to both minimise unwanted currents in the sense wires while also giving the required pulse timing characteristics so that the data latch timing would be correct.

The low component count also means that we will not have any issues when we need to create 16 of these circuits.

The circuit shown in figure 8-1 was used for initial testing and includes switch on rate control but it would not be suitable for the high speed operation that I was looking for and so with that in mind I redesigned the circuit to greatly improve its switching performance.

I spent some time optimising this design to ensure that it matched the drive requirements of the intended system. A key element in its design was ensuring that the switching of the current output transistors was very rapid and we would not be hampered by slow switch off times.

I also designed the circuit such that the current flowing through the wires during the 'on' state was limited to the required amplitude which would produce the correct coincidence switching levels.

Once I had fully tested this new design I turned it into a bridge circuit as shown in figure 8-2 which is really just two of the driver circuits arranged back to back.

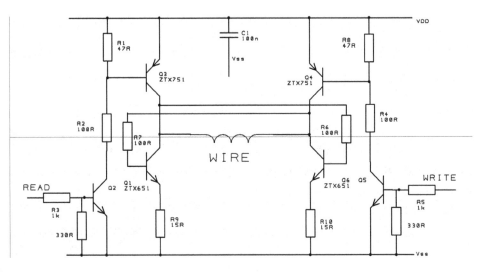

Figure 8-2 Wire Driver Bridge Circuit

In the circuit shown in figure 8-2 we can control the direction of the current flowing in the load by selectively asserting either the READ or the WRITE inputs as long as we are careful not to take them both high at the same time although the circuit does have inherent current limiting should that occur. The current through the load is then controlled by the resistor R9 or R10. When selecting values for these components we must remember that we are trying to control the current through the X and Y selection wires and so if you use a scope to look at the signals at each end of the wire it may seem odd but examining the current flowing in the wire will show that the circuit provides the required pulse control.

Power dissipation in the driver circuit is very low due to the fast switching speed and only operating the drivers in their fully on or fully off states. Not only does this keep the average power drawn by the system very low but it also means that we do not need to concern ourselves with thermal control considerations for the driver circuits other than making sure each was closely thermally coupled to the board inner power planes which.

Note that I am designing this circuit so that it will operate properly when a control pulse of 400nS in duration is applied to one of the two control inputs. Switching of any core flux states will normally be completed within approximately 320nS from the start of the pulse so this timing gives us a good safety margin.

Although we will require 16 of these bridge circuits we will only ever be driving two of them at the same time and so the maximum peak current from the power supply will only be approximately 600mA (not including the inhibit currents).

When designing this circuit I wanted to be able to drive all 16 X and Y selection drivers using common control lines so that I would not need to include pre-drivers for the driver output stages. This would have been needed if we tried driving the output transistors directly because the transistors have limited current gain and trying to drive many such devices from a common control line would have caused problems.

This is why Q2 and Q5 are included in the circuit in figure 8-2 as these effectively provide much higher overall current gain for the driver and it will in fact give reasonable switching speeds with control line source impedances of up to 22k. This means that we can easily switch these driver circuits using common control lines which are derived directly from the outputs of TTL devices without the need for further current drivers.

This was one of my main design goals when considering the overall system development. I wanted to separate the operation of the current driver circuits and sense amplifiers from the control logic as this would allow a much more straight forward design.

It should be noted here that the level of drive current which the wire drivers produce affect not just the switch or no switch states of the ferrite cores but also the level of the output signal when a core actually changes state. As I stated previously the design of a magnetic core memory system is a collection of sub systems which all interact and so designing the system logically is important.

The final design step for the selection pulse generation circuit is to add a pulse strobe circuit which will allow us to selectively apply a current in either direction through required X and Y wires for the specified pulse duration.

Slow pulse turn off or excessive noise in the drive circuits would cause erratic operation of the system and so must be avoided.

By designing the driver circuits so that they can easily be controlled directly from TTL output stages we can now easily crate a control system which uses common strobe lines for the READ and WRITE drivers.

Note that the terms READ and WRITE in this context refer to the internal memory cycles and not the host system read and write operations.

The circuit must achieve several objectives including the generation of either read or write pulses depending on the current mode of operation of the memory system and it must also allow us to determine which X and Y selection lines are to be pulsed.

I wanted to use a single pulse generator for all 16 X and Y selection lines because by doing this it would not only simplify the overall design but it would also remove the possibility of race conditions occurring between the different pulse generators.

Using a single pulse sequence generator would guarantee that all the drivers received exactly the same timing control signals and while this does not allow for differences in the core characteristics it does simplify the design and the sense amplifiers were designed in such a way that variations in core performance could be accounted for by correctly adjusting the amplifier thresholds.

If the select and inhibit wires are not accurately current controlled and correctly timed then the memory cores will receive incorrect control currents and the system will fail to operate correctly.

Also by optimising the drive circuits we can maximise the outputs from the sense amplifiers without the risk of unstable system behaviour.

As we develop our core memory system we will need to design a set of circuits which work together in order to generate some fairly complex and critically timed behaviour. While creating complex control sequences would be very easy it we simply dropped in a modern microcontroller and wrote a few lines of code I do not intend to take that approach. While it could be argued that using TTL is making this task unnecessarily difficult it would be just as valid to say that using core memory in place of something like an SD card is also taking the more difficult approach. I am hoping that the reader selected this book because they are interested in the technologies which were available back before microprocessors were throw away commodities.

I also think it will be far more interesting to develop our system using discrete devices although this does not mean adding circuit complexity just for the sake of it.

In fact I believe that a great deal can be learned by trying to design efficient circuits rather than just adding additional layers each time a new function is required so if we can derive our system features through design rather than simply adding more devices then I hope it will result in a more elegant final solution.

As each new control step is added to our design I will attempt to keep the overall design as clean and concise as possible and not just jump straight to adding more components.

During the testing of the ferrite core and the selection line driver circuits I was using a drive pulse width of 400nS and you will not be surprised when I say that this was not a random choice. The required memory read latch delay is 400nS from the start of the read or write pulse and so in a previous chapter we designed a pulse time delay circuit which gave us the required 400nS delay before it generated the falling edge for the latch enable input to the read buffer latch.

This means that we already have a 400nS high level pulse which is triggered to start by the start of read or start of write trigger signal.

We can therefore use this same pulse to drive the selection wire strobe pulse which we will use in both memory read and memory write modes.

This will again eliminate the need for additional circuits as well as ensuring that our relative timing remains correct. After all it can hardly drift when the same pulse is being used to provide both functions.

So the next question is how to provide strobe pulses to the correct wire drivers based on the required target memory address.

In chapter 5 we discussed a memory decoder which took the 6 bit memory address and decoded it to select one of the 8 available X wires and one of the 8 available Y wires. We will therefore use these 16 select lines to control a series of gates in order to supply a strobe pulse to the correct X and Y wire current pulse drivers.

Each wire driver comprises of a bridge circuit which is controlled by one of two inputs. By driving either of these two inputs high we can create a current pulse in the wire in whichever direction we choose for either reading or writing the memory.

All we need to do is determine how to correctly strobe the correct two lines, one X and one Y, for 400nS. The 400nS timing signal will come from the pulse generator circuit already mentioned.

Although the memory must provide both read and write cycles it is important to note that both of these cycles actually consist of a read phase followed by a write phase and so we need to design a control system to generate both a read strobe and a write strobe in sequence. We will look at the actual pulse sequence generator later but first we need to design a gating circuit to control the drivers.

This will make interfacing to the X and Y drivers very simple as it isolates the need for the control logic to deal with the wire drivers directly and it can control them using a single strobe line.

The circuit in figure 8-3 shows how we can use a few AND gates to convert the two strobe pulses into one of four control lines to give us XRead, XWrite, YRead and YWrite strobe lines. Each one of these lines will pulse high for 400nS at the appropriate time depending on the current memory mode and phase.

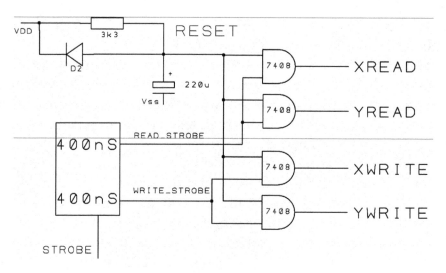

Figure 8-3 Wire Read/Write Selection Circuit

The observant reader may have realised that technically we could combine these four lines into just two and simply use something such as ZYRead and XYWrite.

However we need to drive 16 select strobe gates and although 74ls TTL device outputs should be able to drive up to 20 74ls TTL inputs I was not happy to do that as it would take us too close to the limit and in particular we have fairly strict timing requirements and overloading TTL outputs can cause unpredictable behaviour. I therefore decided to split the 16 lines into two groups of 8 and although I could have divided these in any arbitrary way I though it made most sense to split them in a logical manner.

This circuit also performs another very important function which I will describe here although it really relates to the overall system design and function.

The circuits we will be using to drive the X and Y selection wires are designed using bipolar transistors and these are in turn directly controlled from TTL logic gate outputs. An important consideration whenever developing mixed technology systems such as this is that while each individual circuit may work very well in isolation this may not be the case when they are combined in a complex system.

The magnetic core memory system we are designing here may only have 64 bytes of data storage capacity but it still requires a complex set of control circuits in order to make it function correctly.

The wire driver circuits described earlier are full bridge driver circuits as so it is important that the two control inputs are never taken high at the same time. If both inputs are driven high at the same time then they will effectively short circuit the positive supply rail directly to the 0V rail through two parallel 15R resistors. The total load on the 5V power supply would therefore be in excess of 10A which would not be desirable.

Once the system is running this situation cannot happen because the control logic uses a 'mutually exclusive' design in which single control lines determine the state of the two control inputs that are connected to each wire driver bridge.

However it should be remembered that as TTL logic devices are powered up their outputs may momentarily take on output states which are not defined by the normal logic function of the device. While this transient condition should only last a few nano seconds it can cause trouble under certain conditions. In our design the control inputs to the bridge driver circuits only require around 0.5V in order to turn on and this voltage may easily be exceeded during system power up when the TTL logic gates controlling them are still in their transient state.

This will most likely result in both sides of the wire driver bridge turning on at the same time and forming what is an almost dead short circuit to 0V. There are also 16 of these bridge drivers in our design and so as stated above the combined current they could pass is very large and would almost certainly result in the power supply failing to rise to a level where the TTL devices function as they should.

The overall result would be that the system would almost certainly fail to power up correctly and would possibly destroy itself or the power supply in the process.

The circuit shown in figure 8-3 has a second function which is to eliminate the possibility of the bridge circuits malfunctioning during the power up phase.

It should be noted here that another solution could be to use separate power supplies for the logic and current driver circuits.

I decided not to do this for two reasons and the first of these is because as I already mentioned I wanted to use a single power supply.

The second reason is more to do with good design practices and although using a separate power supply may allow the system to power up successfully there would still be a short time during each power up where the TTL circuits are likely to cause both sides of the wire driver bridge circuits to turn on at the same time and even if they ultimately recovered this would represent a bad design. In fact to avoid this type of situation many older systems used power supply systems which had sequenced power up for each rail.

For our system all the problems associated with the power up of the bridge circuits could be eliminated by the simple inclusion of a reset delay circuit between the decoder and driver circuits.

Note that this cannot be in the form of a TTL timer circuit because it would suffer the same transient power up problems. Instead I added a second function to the strobe control gates and in figure 8-3 you can see that a short delay is created using a resistor and capacitor to disable the bridge driver gates for approximately 750mS following initial power up. The diode provides a fast discharge for the capacitor during power down so that the reset circuit is ready for another power up immediately following a power down.

It is important that these parts are fitted prior to powering up the memory system otherwise damage may occur to the wire driver circuits or power supply.

Many other solutions could be put in place to deal with this type of problem but it is always worth considering power up and transient states when designing systems.

In this case I selected a very simple solution which avoided the need to add additional circuitry other than a few discrete components. Alternatively I could have modified the bridge circuits to make their control inputs mutually exclusive but as there are 16 of these circuits and I already needed the strobe control gates then it was an easy decision to use these gates to add the power up protection.

Once the power up delay has completed then the strobe control gates function as simple buffers and can be used to provide the four control strobe lines to the wire driver control gates.

This circuit also protects the memory system from accidental 'writes' during the power up process. If any of the bridge circuits are inadvertently activated during the power up phase then it is possible that one or memory cores could have their magnetisation states altered and although this memory system is not intended as a commercial grade design it is still good design practice to avoid unwanted system behaviour.

As we already have the decoded X and Y driver lines available all we need to do now is to use a single AND gate for each required control line to act as a strobe gate and we will have everything in place that we need to set the Read / Write control line and then on the next trigger rising edge the selected memory cores will be strobed through the X and Y wires with a 400nS current pulse.

If we are in read mode then the resulting data which is read from the memory cores will also be saved in the memory read buffer latch.

Figure 8-4 shows part of the circuit for driving the select lines and in total there are 32 of these lines to control.

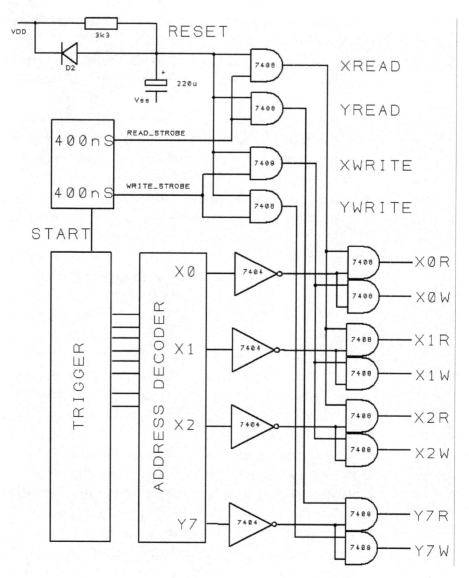

Figure 8-4 Selection Wire Strobe Control Circuit

At initial power application the gates are prevented from activating the wire driver circuits by the 3k3 resistor and 220uF capacitor. These components provide approximately 1 second hold following power up during which time the line drivers are forced to be inactive. This in turn prevents any spurious pulses appearing on the wire driver outputs and also ensures that the current drawn during power up is properly controlled. D2 is included to rapidly discharge the 220uF capacitor when power is removed and so the reset hold circuit is re-enabled very quickly after power off.

The overall design I am trying to achieve is to isolate the actual driving of the memory cores from the higher level control logic by creating a set of sub systems which the control logic can simply use to perform the higher level memory system operations. This means that issues such as the specific pulse timing and ferrite core response times do not need to be taken care of by the higher control logic as the lower level sub systems handle the finer details of driving the magnetic cores.
This should not only make the overall system more reliable but also makes its operation easier to explain and will allow much more scope for developing the system further in future.

Although I have not shown it on the schematics we will need to include good power rail isolation and decoupling for each part of the electronic control system because we are generating a lot of high current pulsed control circuits which all have specific timing requirements. Some of the signals we are trying to detect are also of very low amplitude and so this combination requires some careful consideration in the design of the electronics and I will give some more specific details on this in later chapters.
I decided to use 4 layer boards for the control and driver circuits as this enabled me to design a system with very favourable power supply distribution characteristics.

We still need to develop a lot of control sequence logic before the memory system will operate correctly but we have now created a sub system which will allow us to concentrate on the required logic and leave the details of how to drive the magnetic core up to the circuits we have now designed.

Actually before we can move on to the control logic system there is one more aspect of driving the core that we need to take care of as we will be unable to successfully write data values into the memory without it. We need some way to drive the inhibit lines and so in the next chapter we will design a suitable inhibit wire driver.

It is worth spending a little time here considering the currents selected for the X, Y and inhibit drivers because the values chosen are possibly not as obvious as you may expect.

Firstly we have so far only really considered the simple configuration of a single core with the 3 wires passing through it. However this is not how the actual array is constructed and the requirements are considerably more complex than they may first appear.

We must remember that the inhibit wire actually passes through all 64 cores in each array mat and each mat is responsible for storing individual bits within each byte. That is bit 0 in each byte is stored in mat 0 and bit 1 is stored in mat 1 and so on.

Also remember that the X wires pass through 8 cores in each mat so for example the X0 wire passes through all X0 cores in each mat and so it passes through a total of 64 cores. The same is true for the Y wires which also all pass thorough 64 cores each.

In an earlier chapter we looked at the direct coupled signal created when the X and Y selection wire current pulses are generated. In reality the coupling is much greater than I showed because of the number of coupled cores on each sense wire.

In addition the signal from the sense wire is reduced because the wire passes through 64 cores and only one of these cores is generating an output signal.

The outcome of all this is that the output signal is very small compared to the direct coupled signals and other noise and this is why I spent so much time optimising the ability of the system to discriminate between the direct coupled pulses and the output signal pulses.

You may recall that the method used is to discriminate between the direct coupled X and Y selection wire currents and the core magnetisation switching signals by sampling the output from the sense wire at a specific time. This is also implemented in order to give much more consistent switch times for the ferrite cores when the current pulses are applied. Without consistent switching from the wire drivers the point at which the cores switched state would be unpredictable and being very close to the large direct coupled spikes it would make discrimination of the wanted signal difficult or even impossible considering that all the cores may not switch at exactly the same time.

In order to keep the overall circuits as simple as possible and bearing in mind that the system uses a single 5 volt power supply the selection current pulse amplitudes are determined by a single series resistor.

I should point out here that we must also design the response of the sense amplifier such that it properly matches the output signals from the sense wires which the selection drive currents will create.

In normal operation the X and Y selection drivers turned on long enough for the current in the wire to reach saturation before it turns off again and so the values indicated in the schematics may not appear to match those indicated when we considered the required switching currents for the cores we are using but the current control rates and pulse width must be taken into account.

To further complicate the picture we should also remember that the inhibit wire driver is not a bridge circuit and so actually applies a slightly higher voltage to the inhibit wire than the X and Y bridge driver circuits. We therefore need to use a larger resistor value for this circuit than is used in the X and Y driver circuits. We also must ensure that the inhibit driver turns on slightly faster than the X and Y driver circuits to avoid the possibility of the core values changing due to the inhibit wire current pulse occurring after the selection wire driver current pulses.

Due to the number of cores and interaction between the cores and wires the actual required resistor values are within a 5-8% range and so if you wish to experiment with the system performance then this should be remembered.

As I mentioned earlier the final design for this system uses a different technique for driving the select wires and so the design of the sense amplifier and inhibit driver needed to be developed to properly match the operation of the wire drivers.

If you decide to design your own magnetic core memory system then I strongly advise you to select the general functional technique which you intend to use as it makes a very significant difference to the design of the various circuits.

ℰℊℐℰ

Chapter 9 – Inhibit Driver

In the previous chapter we developed a pulse generator circuit for the memory core X and Y selection lines and in this chapter we will design a circuit for the inhibit line driver.

Luckily the design for the inhibit driver circuits can be less complex than the X and Y selection wire drivers because it only ever needs to generate a current pulse in a single direction. It does however need to provide correctly timed currents of the correct amplitude because the current pulses must be generated accurately or the memory cores could switch magnetisation states when they are not intended to. It also needs to share a common wire with the sense amplifier and so we must design a circuit that will not prevent detection of the small amplitude sense signals.

Before we look at the inhibit driver circuit I will just recap on the purpose of the inhibit line and what the drive requirements will be.

To understand why we need the inhibit line and what drive requirements it has we must expand a little on the inner workings of a core memory system.

In this type of system we do not individually control each separate memory core as this would require a very large number of driver circuits. Instead we arrange them into arrays and individual cores are selected within the array by two coincidence currents flowing in wires which pass through a particular core.

Only the core which has two active current carrying wires passing through it will change its magnetisation state and any cores which have no current carrying wires or just a single current carrying wire will remain unchanged. If for example we pass currents through conductors in row X3 and column Y2 then the core at location X3,Y2 will be set to the '1' state.

The meaning of the term, '1' state, simply refers to a core which has been magnetised in a particular polarity and is an arbitrary design decision as to which direction that will be and is not an inherent property of the ferrite cores.

There is however an important implication in this method of addressing the cores which is that we can only change the cores from a '0' state to a '1' state. We cannot set some cores to a '1' state at the same time as we set others to a '0' because the wire passing through row X3 on mat 0 is the same wire which passes through row X3 on all the other mats. Naturally we cannot pass a current in both directions at the same time so we have to find a way to write values such as 10101010 to the selected memory address.

If we simply selected all 8 bits where each of the bits is on separate array mats then we would end up setting all 8 bits to a '1' state to give 11111111 which is of course not what we want to do.

We could of course design the system so that each mat had its own set of X and Y wire driver circuits but this would be impractical. Each mat in our small system has an 8 x 8 array of cores and so it requires 8 X wire drivers and 8 Y wire drivers giving a total of 16 driver circuits. Each of these circuits must be capable of driving currents through the selection wires in both directions. If each mat required a separate set of driver circuits then even a system as small as ours would need a total of 128 driver circuits instead of just 16.

Therefore the added complexity of arranging the cores into arrays and using inhibit wires is introduced. The advantage of this technique becomes even more significant as memory size grows.

Inhibit Wire Function

This is where the inhibit wire is used.

As I explained in an earlier chapter there is an inhibit wire which passes through all the cores on each mat to give a total of 8 inhibit wires for the entire system. If we pass a current through selection wires X3 and Y2 then the cores at this location on all 8 mats would change state to a '1' but if at the same time we pass a current in the opposite direction through the inhibit wire on mat 1 for example then the result would be to set the value 11111101 in the memory at address X3,Y2.

By selectively driving the inhibit wires we can cause any value we require to be 'written' into the required memory address.

There is however still a problem which we must overcome before this will work. Let us assume that the memory at address X3,Y2 currently has a value stored in it of:

00001111

And we try to write a value of:

11110000

Then we will actually end up with a value of:

11111111

Stored at that address which is of course the incorrect.

This will happen because we can only actively write bit values of '1' to the core or prevent (inhibit) the writing of a '1' to the cores.

We are not actually writing '0' values but are simply avoiding or inhibiting the writing of '1's.

To overcome this the memory write process is actually a two step process in which we begin by erasing the current memory address by writing '0's to all 8 cores before we write the new value to the same address.

In the above example the memory at address X3,Y2 would be updated as follows.

00001111

Would be erased to:

00000000

And then the value of:

11110000

Would be written to the memory location using the inhibit wires on mats 0,1,2,3 to prevent '1's being written to the first 4 bits.

We do not actually need to add more circuits for the erase function because as you no doubt recall all that is required is for us read the memory at the required address before we write the new value into that address. This works because the read function will always result in the selected memory address being cleared to a value of 00000000 by the read operation. We can simply ignore the value which we have read out of memory if we are performing a write cycle.

Now that we know what the purpose of the inhibit line is we must determine what amplitude the current pulse to drive it must be.

The total current required to change the magnetisation state of a core in our system is around 700mA and is provided by coincidence currents in two separate conductors where each conductor is carrying half the total current of 350mA. We do not want to pass the full 700mA through the inhibit wire because it passes through all the cores in its mat and this would cause all the cores in the mat to switch magnetisation state. Instead we can pass a current which is equal in magnitude to the current in one of the selection wires but opposite in polarity through the inhibit wire.

This will result in the total coincidence current in the selected core being effectively reduced to the equivalent of a single wire current and so the core will remain in its un flipped state and as it was cleared to a '0' before the write then it will remain at zero.

We now know that we must drive the inhibit wire with a current of 350mA in the opposite direction to the selection wires when in write mode.

In fact we can reduce the current amplitude required in the inhibit wire to a lower value as we only require sufficient current to prevent the coincidence currents reaching the critical level.

Reducing the current in the inhibit wire will result in a significant reduction in peak current drawn by the system.

The inhibit wires are only used when writing a '0' to the core but if a value such as 00000000 is being written then this of course requires that all 8 inhibit wires need to be energised and the result is a very large current spike. By reducing the current in the inhibit wire we can minimise the amplitude of the current spike while retaining the function of the inhibit wire.

I have found that a current of just 200mA is sufficient to provide the inhibit function but to allow a safety margin I decided to use 240mA.

We also know that we only need to pass a current through the inhibit wire in one direction and so a very simple driver circuit can be used and this is shown in figure 9-1.

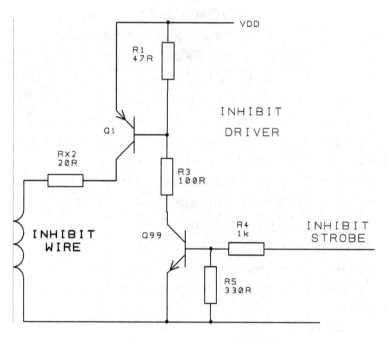

Figure 9-1 Inhibit Driver Circuit

In the circuit shown in figure 9-1 I have shown the inhibit driver circuit and as you can see it is a very simple design although it still has very good switching characteristics. It also has a very important design feature in that one end of the inhibit wire is connected to the 0V power rail and we will see why that is important shortly.

It should be noted here that most commercial systems except very early ones used the same wire for both the inhibit and sense functions which works very well as these two functions are never required at the same time and this arrangement makes the construction of the core much easier but the control electronics is more complex.

In this memory development project I have specifically designed the overall layout of the memory core so that we can easily combine the sense and inhibit functions into a single wire and thus remove the need to thread separate inhibit wires through the memory cores. All of the explanations given so far are still valid for either combined sense and inhibit functions or if the two functions are performed using a single wire but we need to design our circuits accordingly.

In larger commercial systems a multi rail power supply was generally used and this allows for much easier control of the required current pulse generator circuits. It does however also generally require isolation transformers for all of the driver circuits along with dual polarity control.

As I decided to design this system using a single 5V power supply rail then a great deal of the complexity could be designed out although this does introduce other difficulties.

If we take another look at the sense amplifier, shown in figure 9-2, which we designed in chapter 7 then we can see that one end of the sense wire is connected to 0V and as I mentioned above this is an important part of the system design.

If we then look back at the circuit shown in figure 9-1 we can see that one end of the inhibit wire is also connected to ground.

This is no coincidence and I specifically arranged the two circuits this way to enable us to combine the sense and inhibit functions into a single wire configuration.

By designing the sense amplifier circuit and the inhibit driver circuit in such a way that both required one end of the inhibit / sense wire to be connected to ground then a lot of design complications could be avoided.

This does make design of the sense amplifier a little more difficult as we must then detect a very low amplitude signal in a wire which is connected directly to 0V.

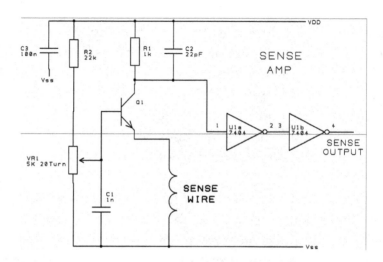

Figure 9-2 Sense Amplifier Circuit

As I mentioned earlier the sense and inhibit functions are never active at the same time and so looking at the circuits in figures 9-1 and 9-2 it is clear that we can simply connect both circuits together and use a single sense / inhibit wire as shown in figure 9-3.

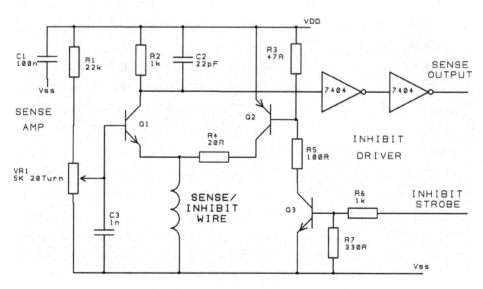

Figure 9-3 Combined Sense Amp and Inhibit Driver

In this circuit sense amplifier works exactly as it did previously and as the inhibit driver transistor, Q2, is turned off during a read cycle then it has very little impact on the output of the sense amplifier.

During a write cycle when the inhibit driver may be active the sense amplifier output is ignored and so the two functions can operate independently using this circuit and we can eliminate the need for a separate inhibit wire. We have not actually added any components in order to achieve this and so this represents a very good solution to this particular design problem.

It is worth pointing out here that combining these two functions in larger commercial magnetic core memory systems is a little more difficult because of the nature of the circuits employed but the extra effort required to design suitable electronics to cater for this is more than made up for by removing the need for the separate inhibit wires which in large core memory systems may have to be threaded through many thousands of cores. It also of course means that we can use thicker wire for the remaining 3 conductors because of the space freed up by removing the fourth wire and with the tiny ferrite cores which were used in these systems that really made a big difference to the practicality of manufacturing these arrays.

As with the other parts of the development I want to complete the design of this sub system by adding the interface circuits which will enable the inhibit drivers to be easily accessed by the control logic without the control circuits needing to concern themselves with the details of the inner workings of the inhibit drivers.

In order to do that we need to add an interface to our inhibit drivers which will only need to be supplied with the current data value to be written and a strobe signal. In fact we want to be able to use the same strobe signal which is used to trigger the X and Y selection drivers because this will then guarantee the correct relative timing is maintained during a core write cycle which is when the inhibit drivers are needed.

If you recall the selection strobe pulse is a high level pulse with a duration of 400nS and we will use that same signal to control the inhibit drivers.

This is actually a very easy circuit to implement because all it needs us to do is gate the data value which is to be written into the memory core in such a way that when the strobe input is low all the inhibit drive lines are also low. When the strobe line is high then any data bits which are low need to generate an inhibit pulse and so the circuit must set these bits to a high value for the duration of the strobe pulse. Any data bits which are high must result in the inhibit lines remaining inactive so that the '1' values are written into the core.

Figure 9-4 shows the circuit for this decoding function and it is simply comprised of eight NOR gates and an inverter. The inverter generates the required low strobe pulse and each of the NOR gates is used to control one of the data lines.

I mentioned previously that it was important that the inhibit and X,Y driver circuit timing were all timed correctly relative to each other and this decoder circuit is part of that timing.

If you examine the X and Y wire control logic circuits and then compare this to the inhibit wire control logic you will see that the overall timing means that the inhibit drivers will begin to switch a few nano seconds prior to the X and Y drivers.

By arranging the system in this manner we can be sure that inadvertent switching of memory cores will be avoided and the memory arrays will be driven in a reliable fashion.

It is actually unlikely that a few nano seconds either way would make much difference as the cores require significant time to switch state but as proper timing is good design then I decided to make sure the control circuits all played well together.

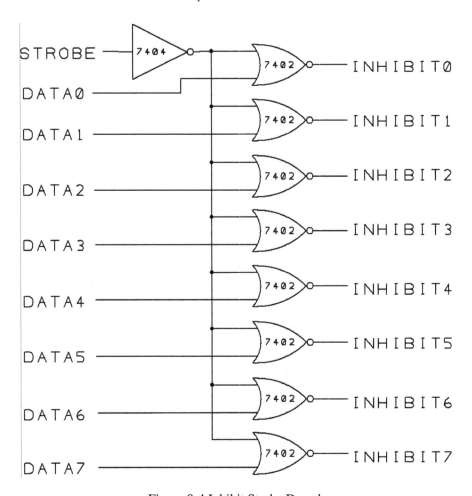

Figure 9-4 Inhibit Strobe Decoder

In this and the previous few chapters we have put together a collection of methods and circuits which we can now use to complete the design of our magnetic core memory system. By separating each major function and creating circuits which handle these functions automatically we can now turn our attention to designing the control logic circuit which will generate the sequences of control signals required to turn our assortment of core sub systems into a fully working ferrite core magnetic memory.

Chapter 10 – Control Logic

It is now time to take the sub systems we have designed in the earlier chapters of this book and link them all together using a logic control circuit to produce a fully functional magnetic core memory system. As we progress through the design in this chapter it will hopefully become clear why I included the interface control logic in each of the sub systems because by doing so it makes our job of designing the control logic circuits much more straight forward. Now of course it could be argued that technically all the logic elements we have designed so far are actually part of the system control logic. However by conceptually dividing the system in discrete functional blocks where each block has a clearly defined interface then the design process is easier and generally results in a less complex solution.

If we take the inhibit driver which we designed in the previous chapter then all it requires is an 8 bit data value and a strobe pulse and so from the design perspective all we need to do to make use of it is connect it to the correct data source and provide a strobe pulse at the correct time. This is much easier to put into a development context than having to deal with the timing and drive signals required to control the inhibit wire currents. Another benefit in taking this approach to project management is that if you are running a larger development with a number of engineers all working on the same design then by defining an interface for each sub system along with any required timing and drive characteristics then each designer knows what they are supposed to be designing. This is far more likely to result in a well organised development program than one in which there are no clearly defined interfaces between each part of the system. It also allows very specific testing to be carried out on each part of the system before it is added to the overall design and that is exactly the approach I used here.

Before we begin designing the control logic circuits it may be useful to review exactly what we need them to achieve as this will effectively provide a way to define our control logic parameters.

There are three main modes that the memory system will be required to provide and these are as follows:

1) Idle – In this mode the memory is not performing any task.
2) Read – The memory retrieves data from the supplied address.
3) Write – Data is saved into memory at the supplied address.

If we now expand on each of these to see what is required and how each sub system will be used then we will be able to create a list of operations for each required mode.

Idle Mode

In idle mode the memory will not be driving the data bus and so needs to put its data output buffer into a high impedance state.

No internal operations will be carried out in this mode although any which have been started prior to the memory entering idle mode must be completed to avoid the possibility data loss.

For this mode the easiest solution is to use the RW control input to directly control the data output buffer so that in read mode the data bus is an output and in write mode it is an input.

It is however important that if the memory is performing an internal task then it completes this task before changing state unless the internal process is fully independent to the data bus. I will come back to this later.

Write Mode Sequence

In write mode the control logic needs to perform the following tasks:

1) Latch the Address bus into the X,Y decoder.
2) Perform a dummy read to erase the current memory location.
3) Use a multiplexer to connect the inhibit drivers to the data bus.
4) Provide strobe pulses to the Inhibit and X,Y drivers.

These requirements show that we will need a 6 bit latch to store the supplied address. We may be able to get away without using a latch for the memory address although there is a danger in that case that the address may change during the write process and this would result in possible loss of data. By latching the address into a latch before the memory write process is started we can be confident that the memory will use the correct address throughout the process.

I would also add at this point that I included sufficient bulk capacitance on the control board so that it would be able to complete the current memory cycle should power be interrupted during the process.

Most commercial magnetic core memory systems used a similar approach in order to avoid data loss and it was normally provided in the form of very large capacitors in the power supplies. Designers recognised the importance of data protection very early in the development of computer systems and core memory is very robust in this sense.

Read Mode Sequence

Read mode is actually very similar to write mode because as I stated previously the action of reading the memory cores actually erases them in what is termed a destructive read. We must therefore restore the contents of a memory location following any read. In many commercial systems there was an option to skip the write back part of this process if the host system intended to alter the memory contents immediately following the read. For example if the memory location held a counter that needed to be incremented then the host system only needed to read the current value and then increment it and then write the new value back to the same location. This implies that there is no need to restore the original data value because it will not be needed again and by skipping the re-write phase of the process the memory could operate more quickly.

I will not be implementing that feature although it would be relatively simple to add should the reader wish to further develop this system.

This means that our system must perform the following steps during a memory read cycle.

1) Latch the Address bus into the X,Y decoder.
2) Read the data from memory (this erases the data).
3) Use a multiplexer to connect the inhibit drivers to the read data buffer.
4) Provide strobe pulses to the Inhibit and X,Y drivers (this re-writes the erased data back into memory).
5) Put the data read from memory which is now in the read data buffer onto the external data bus.

We now have a good idea what the memory control logic must achieve and in what order these steps must take place although it is worth pointing out that some of these steps can be carried out concurrently and in fact making the data available on the data bus as soon as it has been read is an advantage and so this is how I designed the system.

I mentioned earlier that we need to isolate the inner working of the memory system from the outside world to ensure that it can perform its function in a consistent way and I have already stated that by adding a latch for the supplied address value we can be sure that the correct address is used for the entire memory cycle irrespective of weather it is a read or a write or even if the RW control line changes state during a memory cycle.

The next addition I will make to further enhance the system architecture is a data output tri-state buffer. If we simply connected the data read buffer to the external data bus when the RW line was taken high then the data presented on the data bus would possibly be incorrect as the memory may be performing a re-write phase of a memory cycle in which case we need the data output from the memory read latch to remain unchanged until this process has completed. By adding a second buffer latch between the data read latch and the output data bus we can put data onto the data bus and the data bus can even change without the data being re-written changing. This could happen for example if the memory was performing a memory re-write and the RW line was taken low. This would cause the data value to take on the data value on the external data bus instead of the data value which was read from the memory and which is currently in the data read latch. The most likely outcome would be corruption of the data value.

Adding the second data latch will avoid this problem by isolating the internal data read latch from the external data bus.

If we bring all the elements discussed so far together into a simple system layout diagram then we end up with the memory structure shown in figure 10-1.

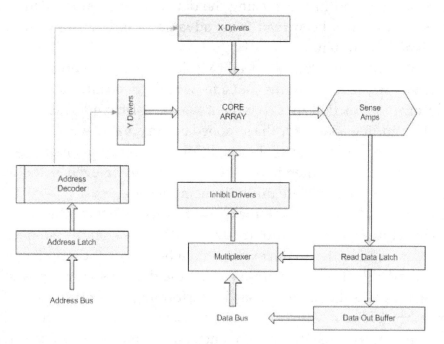

Figure 10-1 Memory System Structure

In this diagram we have all the building blocks which we need in our completed system except for the logic control itself although it is hopefully now clear how the overall system will operate.

In figure 10-1 each major block has either been designed in a previous chapter or is a simple addition using available TTL logic devices such as a data latch or buffer.

What we now need to do is design a control circuit that will take the start signal produced by our start detection circuit which we designed in chapter 6 and then generate a series of correctly timed control signals in order to drive the memory system.

If you recall from the circuit in figure 6-1 from chapter 6 we generate both a high pulse and a low pulse whenever a memory cycle needs to be started. For a commercial system we should include a gate for these signals to prevent a second pulse being generated until the memory has finished its current cycle. This could easily be added using a flip flop which is set when the cycle starts and is cleared at the end of the cycle and when set it inhibits further start pulses from being generated. I will however omit this at the moment in order to keep the circuits as simple as possible but feel free to add this if you decide to build your own version.

The first step in designing the control logic is to decide if we intend to design the memory read or the memory write control first and as the write process starts with a dummy read cycle then it will be easier to start by getting the read cycle working first.

Read Cycle Logic

We can use the state of the RW input to determine which cycle the memory is expected to perform when a start signal is generated although if you look at the list of actions required for the two memory cycles which I presented earlier in this chapter then we can see that the first step is identical for both and so we can begin there. The first step is to latch the provided address into the address latch and we can do this by simply connecting the appropriate start signal to the latch enable pin of the latch. In fact it is even easier that that in this case because if you remember from the trigger circuit design we included the address latch in the trigger circuit and the address is automatically latched whenever it changes. All we need to do is take connections from the output of this latch and we have our internally latched address bus and this is shown in figure 10-2.

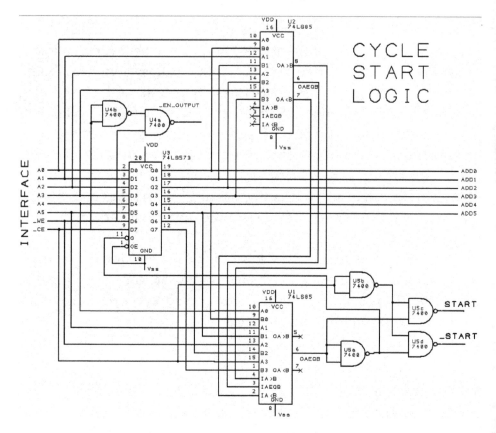

Figure 10-2 Memory Cycle Start Circuit

In this circuit the internal address bus is designated as:
ADD0 to ADD5

The START and _START outputs are the two start cycle trigger pulses which are asserted whenever a memory cycle needs to begin. This occurs automatically if either RW or _CE change or if the memory address changes and this removes the need for any specific memory start signal.

This behaviour makes the overall system operate in a very similar manner to an SRAM memory device.

The board was designed to also allow external START pulses to be provided so that the system could be used with explicit read or write pulse control. I will describe the operation of the board in more detail in a later chapter.

The two gates shown as U4a and U4b are used to generate a control signal for controlling the data bus output buffer. This arrangement causes the internal data latch output to be connected to the external data bus when the memory is enabled and is in read mode. This eliminates the need for additional control logic which would otherwise be needed to determine when the output of the memory system should be active.

In addition by having these gates at the control line inputs then it ensures that the output buffer setup is completed prior to any other actions and so any spurious bus contention is avoided.

The address latch is used to drive the address decoder as discussed in chapter 5 and so we can now add the X and Y decoders to the logic circuit and we then get the circuit shown in figure 10-3.

As I mentioned previously the address latch was included to avoid the possibility of the address being changed during a read or write cycle. By including this latch we can be sure that the address is consistent throughout the entire memory cycle and this avoids the problems which would otherwise occur if the selected address was not stable throughout the memory cycle.

It should also be clear from this diagram how the lower three bits of the address bus are used to select the required X driver and the upper three bits are used to select the Y driver.

It does not really matter if we use a sequential addressing scheme in the design although it does of course make the design and fault finding process far less error prone.

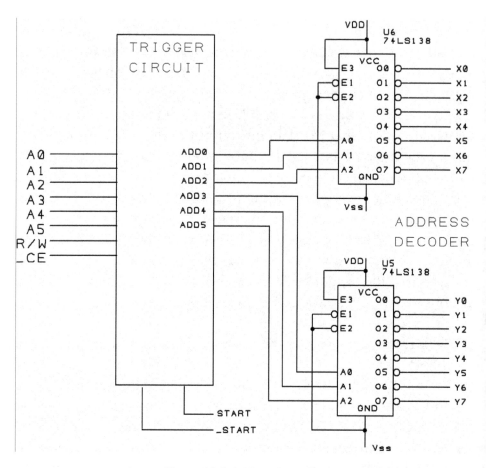

Figure 10-3 Address Decoder

This circuit takes the 6 bit address from the trigger circuit latch and decodes it into an X,Y core location which is then fed to the X and Y wire selection driver circuits.

The supplied address is effectively split into two three bit values with one value being decoded as the X line and the other as the Y line. Each of these three bit values is decoded to select either one of eight X wires or one of eight Y wires.

Remember here that the X and Y driver circuits only need to select cores based on the supplied memory address. It is the task of the inhibit circuits to handle the actual data value which is to be written. The outputs from the address decoders are therefore fed directly to the driver control logic circuits.

At first glance it may seem tempting to simply use one of the enable inputs of the 74ls138 devices as the strobe control line for the X and Y wire drivers. However we must remember that we are currently only dealing with the read part of the cycle but the drivers must also handle the write phase of the memory cycle. During the read phase the drivers must pass current through the selection wires in the opposite direction to the write phase. This requires that the driver control circuits actually control 32 inputs to the drivers and not simply the 16 lines from the decoder.

The strobe signal we will use will be generated by a 400nS pulse delay circuit which is triggered by the START pulse.

It is important to note here that the propagation delay in the 74ls138 is only around 30nS and so we can use either the START or the _START pulse directly to strobe the driver circuits because the address decoding will be completed well before the driver circuits have switched on.

As with all hybrid systems which contain a mixture of logic and analogue circuitry it is very important to fully understand the timing requirements of each section of the system if it is to function correctly. This is especially true in a system such as the one we are developing here because it has some very specific timing requirements along with the need to contend with variability in the response of individual magnetic core performance.

Once the strobe pulse is asserted then the selected X and Y current driver circuits will pass a current through the appropriate X and Y core wires and the direction of this current will depend on current phase of the memory cycle.

Although the memory system has a RW input it is important to understand that this cannot be used to control the wire driver current directions. This is because each complete memory cycle actually consists of a read phase followed by a write phase and this is true irrespective of the state of the RW input. In other words the memory system will need to generate properly timed internal phase control signals so that the system will operate correctly.

From this point onwards things start to get slightly complicated but hopefully we can keep the required circuits as simple as possible.
Both the read cycle and the write cycle are actually multi-phase processes and in fact are almost identical. The only real difference is in the way the data bus is handled because in a write cycle the data is supplied from the host data bus and in a read cycle the data is put onto the bus by the memory system.
In both cases we must start by reading the memory once the address latch has been updated and contains the current required memory address value and then we must write data into the memory core.
This two stage process will require that we create a two step logic process and we will do this by daisy chaining two 400nS pulse generators together.
I could of course have designed the system to trigger two concurrent pulse generators each with different time constants but I felt that by daisy chaining the pulse generators I would have better control over the relative timing of each because any errors in shorter pulses are always going to be smaller than for longer duration pulses. The design I show here is therefore intended to reduce the possibility of timing errors caused by component variability and drift.
The first pulse generator will control the read part of the process and the second will control the write phase and the duration for each pulse will be selected to give optimal system operation.

We could easily trigger the second pulse generator directly from the output of the first but we must remember that the memory core is highly inductive and so we will need to allow it time to 'recover' from the read pulse before we generate the write pulse.

The design of the wire driver circuits is also such that the turn off rate of the current pulse is relatively slow at approximately 100nS and this was designed to minimise the cross coupled signals between the X and Y drivers through cores which are on common wires. If the driver turn off times are too short then large current spikes could be induced in the wires and this would increase the 'noise' problems in the core.

I have therefore included a third timer which sits between the output of the read pulse timer and the trigger input of the write pulse timer and this timer has a duration of approximately 350nS.

The values shown in the timer schematic are for a 350nS delay between the read and write pulses and 400nS X and Y wire selection pulse width but in practice we can reduce this to provide a faster overall memory cycle time.

The presence of the delay timer will also make testing of the memory system much easier as we will be able to distinguish more easily between the core behaviour in the read and write phases of the memory cycle. Without this delay the currents generated in the selection and inhibit wires for the read and write phases would overlap and it would be very difficult to observe what is actually occurring in these wires.

Including this delay also ensures that the previously active wire drivers have fully switched off and this is very important.

If the read and write pulses overlap then the current generated in the selected wire between the read and write phase of the memory cycle will be much higher than intended. The result of this would be that even if only a single X or Y wire is active in a particular core the current magnitude in this single wire may be large enough to cause a flux magnetisation state change.

Or to put it another way if the wire selection currents overlap then the memory contents will be corrupted. The same is also true if the system is trying to write a zero to a core by activating the inhibit wire during the write phase of the memory cycle. If the driver currents overlap causing the applied currents to be higher than intended then the current in the inhibit wire may be insufficient to prevent a one being written back into the core and so a '1' will be written instead of a '0'. Again this would result in corruption of the memory contents.

It is therefore clear that the read phase and write phase current pulses must not be allowed to overlap and the inclusion of the intermediate pulse generator is intended to prevent this from occurring.

Figure 10-4 shows the circuit for the pulse generators

In this schematic VR1 is used to set the duration of the first pulse generator and it is effectively the sample timer for the sense amplifier outputs.

I will discuss how to adjust this in a later chapter and although I could have easily replaced this component with a fixed value resistor I decided to include a variable resistor here as it allows far more scope for experimentation and possible further development by anyone wishing to build their own system.

It may also be possible to use the board to drive existing magnetic memory cores instead of the one I designed for this system although the timing and drive requirements may be very different.

By including the ability to adjust the pulse timing and so adjust the sense amplifier sample point it makes any such experimentation much easier.

There is also the possibility that different constructors may build the core assembly in slightly different ways and again this adjustment may be useful to compensate for any changes brought about by assembly variations.

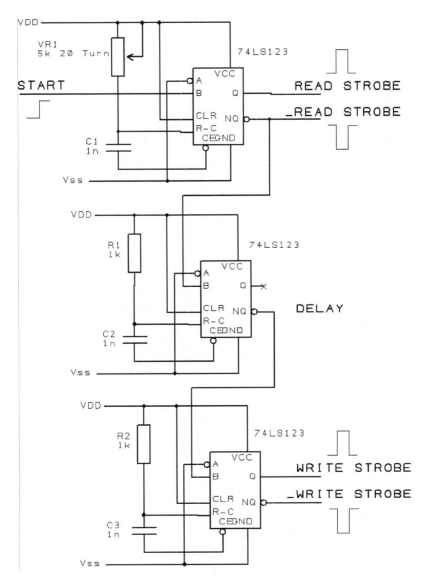

Figure 10-4 Timing Pulse Generator

Each of the timers provides both a high and a low output during the timing pulse and so this will make designing the rest of the logic circuit a little easier. For each phase of the memory cycle process we can just select a suitable timer pulse.

Figure 10-5 shows the circuit with the X and Y driver control gates and reset control.

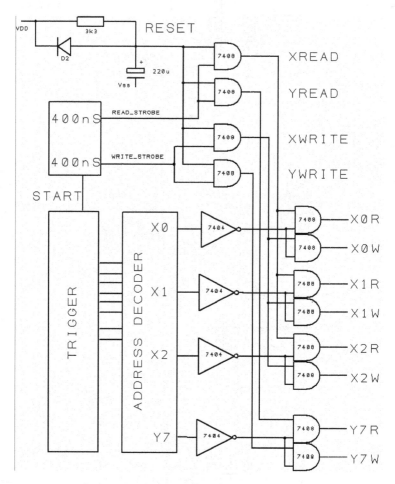

Figure 10-5 X and Y Driver Control Logic

Only a few of the driver control gates are shown but there are actually 32 of these gates in the final design. Only two of the X and Y selection wire drives should be active at any particular time and the reset control circuit ensures all drivers are off during power up. Figure 10-6 shows how the X, Y drivers are connected.

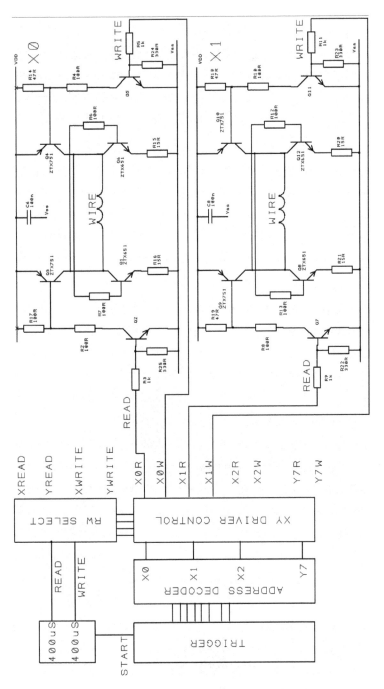

Figure 10-6 Wire Drivers and Control Logic

The total propagation through the address decoder to the strobe control gates will be approximately 60nS but as the time required for triggering the 400nS pulse generator is around 100nS then the address decoding and control gate setup will be completed well before the STROBE pulse arrives.

In figure 10-6 only two drivers are shown but there is one of these for each of the 16 core selection wires. Eight X selection wires and eight Y selection wires.

The READ strobe signal (START) is used to directly control the 'Read Data Latch' and also the X, Y drivers so that by the end of the first pulse generator period the data read from the memory is stored in this latch.

As we are in read mode then this data is made available to the host system by enabling the data output tri-state buffer which puts the data onto the host data bus.

As this occurs immediately following the 400nS read strobe pulse it means that our system has a data access time of around 400nS although the memory cycle time will of course be much longer as it still has work to do before it will be ready for the start of the next memory cycle.

The data which has been read is available at the output of the Read Data Latch which is connected to the data output tri-state buffer but we can also connect this latch to the input of the data multiplexer so that it can be made available to the inhibit control system ready for the write part of the memory cycle.

Because we are in memory read mode the data multiplexer is set to connect the data from the Read Data Latch to the inhibit control circuit.

The circuit for the Read Data Latch, Output Tri-state Buffer and Inhibit Multiplexer is shown in figure 10-7. Both the multiplexer and the tri-state buffer are controlled directly by the RW control line so that they do not need any further control logic.

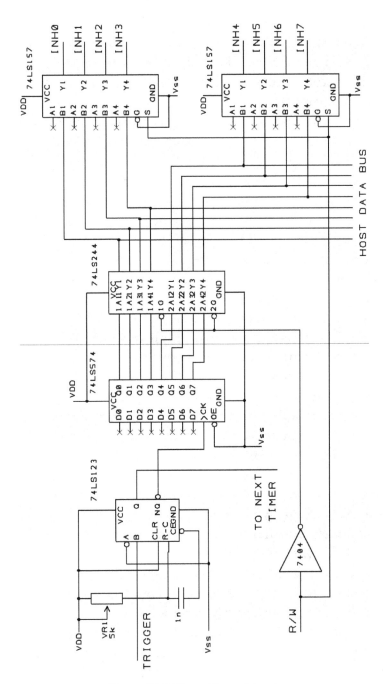

Figure 10-7 Phase Control Logic

In the circuit shown in figure 10-7 the INHx outputs are used to control the inhibit drivers. However they cannot be used directly because the strobe must occur at the correct time in the cycle and also they are currently inverted.

The data fed into the B input of the multiplexer is from the Read Data Buffer which is what we need for the read cycle when the erased data is being written back into the memory. The 74ls157 is a quad 2 input multiplexer and the B inputs are connected to the outputs when the S input is high. This means that it can be controlled directly from the RW control line as we have defined this as being active high when in read mode.

In chapter 9 figure 9-4 showed the inhibit driver strobe control gate circuit and while it may appear that we can eliminate this circuit and simply use the strobe (/G) input of the 74ls157 to perform the same task this unfortunately would not work.

The inhibit drivers must be driven high when a zero value is to be saved into the memory core and so the data values would all need to be inverted. Although the 74ls158 has outputs which are inverted compared to the 74ls157 the outputs are in the high state when the strobe input is inactive and so all the outputs would need to be inverted but then they would be incorrect when passing the data values so we cannot use that method.

We could of course insert inverters between the data bus and the input to the multiplexer but we would need to do the same for the second input when we design the read logic so the simplest solution is to use the circuit shown in figure 9-4 and this is included in the circuit shown in figure 10-8.

Another advantage of using this configuration is that it provides more accurate timing between the X,Y control pulses and the inhibit pulses so the system should operate more reliably.

Note that the second set of inputs to the multiplexers shown in figure 10-8 will be connected to the host data bus to allow data to be selected directly from this data bus during the write cycle.

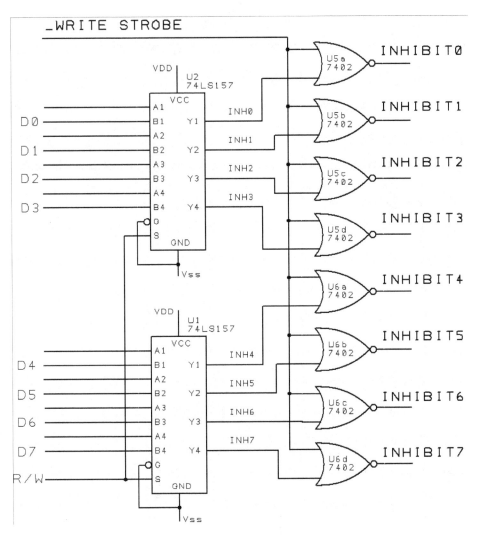

Figure 10-8 Inhibit Strobe Control Circuit

The way this circuit operates is very simple as when the RW line is high the _WRITE STROBE control is used to strobe the inhibit driver gates which are implemented by U5 and U6.

Note that we are using the active low write strobe which is derived from the second (write) 400nS pulse timer.

When the _WRITE STROBE signal pulses low then any high input values present on the B inputs to the multiplexers will propagate to the respective outputs through the control NOR gates and the selected inhibit drivers will be active during the strobe pulse period. Because the same strobe pulse is used for both the X, Y drivers as well as the inhibit drivers then we can be sure that they are properly synchronised. Figure 10-9 shows the circuit with 2 of the 8 inhibit drivers added. The other 6 inhibit drivers are identical. Note that the inhibit driver circuits also include the sense amplifiers although these are only used in the read phase.

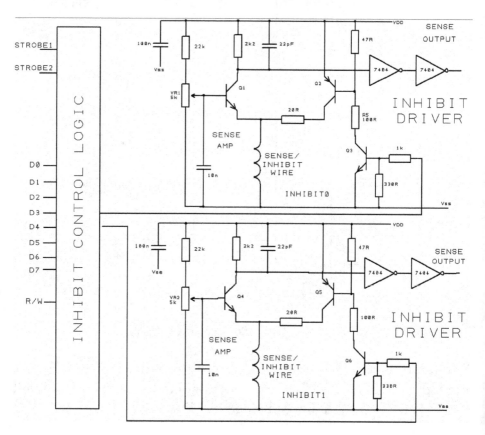

Figure 10-9 Inhibit Control and Driver Circuit

We now have the entire memory read cycle designed and we also have a great deal of the control logic in place which we will need in order to implement the write cycle logic which we will look at next.

Write Mode Logic

The logic required for memory write mode is almost identical to the read cycle except that instead of writing the erased data value back to the memory following the initial read phase we write the current data value present on the host data bus into the memory via the inhibit control and drivers.

The memory system is put into write mode when the RW control input is low and so we can use this line to switch the control logic into the write cycle process.

We have already designed the data read circuits which I showed in the circuit of chapter 7, figure 7-6. The data which is read from the memory when we strobe the X, Y drivers in read mode is stored in the 'Read Data Latch' although for the write cycle dummy read we simply ignore this data value.

The write cycle begins in the same way as the read cycle and so the supplied memory address is saved into the address decoder latch and the read pulse generator is triggered. This causes the data value at the current memory address to be read into the Read Data Buffer and this action also erases the selected memory location. We can ignore the data value which has been read as we simply wanted to erase the memory location which we have now done.

Note that because the RW control input is low the data bus output tri-state buffer is in the high impedance state so it is not trying to put the data value stored in the latch onto the data bus.

Also the RW line being low switches the inhibit multiplexer to the host data bus and so this data becomes available to the inhibit drivers.

During the second 400nS phase of the memory cycle the data value supplied by the host is used by the inhibit drivers to save the correct data value into memory.

The memory write cycle is now complete.

Because we designed the various parts of the memory system to work together it has greatly simplified the logic control development and we have been able to implement a fairly complex task with the minimal number of components and yet we still have a system which has a reasonable level of performance.

Note that switching from read to write mode will disable the tri-state buffer and it will also cause the memory to begin another cycle although it will be at the current address and so the resulting data value will remain unaltered. Depending on your host system architecture it may be preferable to disconnect the RW input from the trigger circuit to prevent changes in RW from starting a cycle.

Although it is probably already clear I will show some simple diagrams to indicate how the data flows through the system for each phase of memory cycle operations.

The two memory cycles are almost identical and only really vary by selecting a different source for the data which is written into the cores during the internal data write phase.

The multiplexers and data buffers work together to direct the flow of data depending on the current phase of the memory cycle and the mode of operation and so the read and write cycles have different data flow paths although the actual cycles are otherwise identical.

Figure 10-10 shows the first phase of the memory read cycle.

In this phase the data is read from the memory core and deposited into the read data buffer (U2) and through the data bus buffer (U3) to the host data bus.

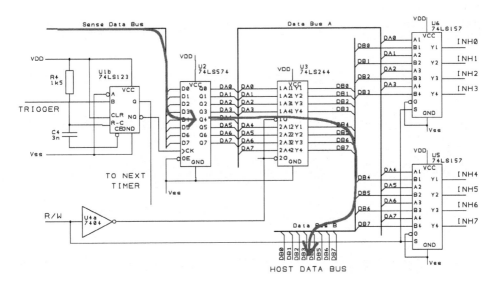

Figure 10-10 Data Flow in Read Phase One

Figure 10-11 shows the data during the restore phase of the read cycle where the data in the read buffer is saved back to memory.

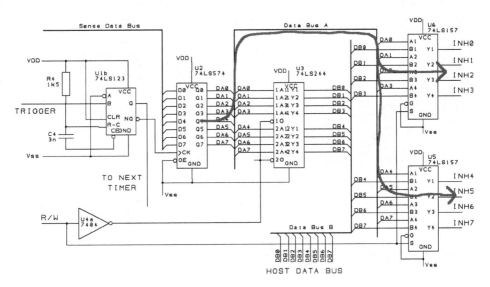

Figure 10-11 Read Phase Data Restore

Figure 10-12 shows the first phase of the memory write cycle where a read from memory erases the current data but this data is ignored.

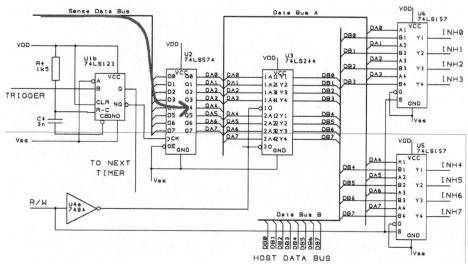

Figure 10-12 First Phase of Write Cycle - Erase

Figure 10-13 shows the second phase of the memory write cycle in which the data on the host data bus is written to the core.

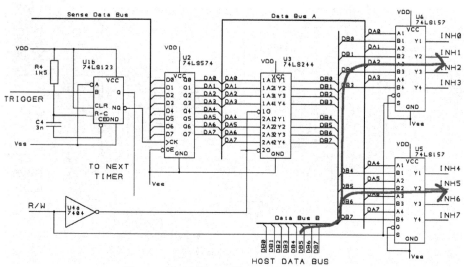

Figure 10-13 Phase Two of Write Cycle

Memory Speed

I did not design this memory system to be high performance so speed of operation was never going to be an issue but it is still worth examining the memory cycle time.

There are two main time values we are interested in when looking at the memory timing. The first of these is the data read access time which is how long it takes from the start of the read memory cycle before the data is available on the host data bus.

While speed was never a design challenge for this system I still wanted to show good design practise for a system of this type and that is why the data buffer puts the data onto the data bus half way through the read cycle. At that time the memory has not completed the full memory cycle but as the data is available immediately following the internal read phase of the cycle it makes the overall host system performance more efficient.

In fact the data read time is just 400nS and although this is incredibly slow compared to modern solid state memory it does compare very well to earlier magnetic core memory systems which used ferrite cores of the type we are using.

The entire memory cycle takes 1.9uS to complete for both the read and write cycles.

I have carried out a few experiments with this memory system and I believe that the speed could be increased to give a memory access time of around 250nS and a cycle time of around 650nS. Again this is not fast by modern standards but it would certainly enable a reasonable host system speed to be achieved.

Of course our memory system only has 64 bytes capacity so it is only intended as an experimental learning tool but anyone that is enthusiastic enough could expand this system to any arbitrary capacity. It should however be noted that as I mentioned previously you would start to encounter various difficulties as the number of cores increased.

ℰℐℰ

Chapter 11 - Testing the Memory

We have now completed the initial magnetic core memory system design and I have turned the various circuits into complete printed circuit board designs and assembled a few units for test purposes. Assembling the actual memory core board was fairly challenging work and if you intent to attempt this then I strongly recommend using a microscope as this makes the entire process much easier. Figure 11-1 shows a close up of one of the core mats and figure 11-2 shows the complete core assembly.

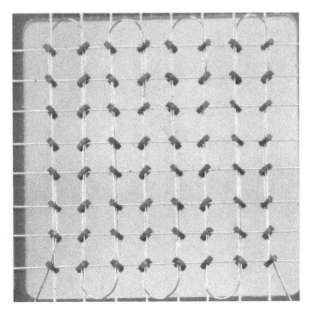

Figure 11-1 A Single Completed Core Mat

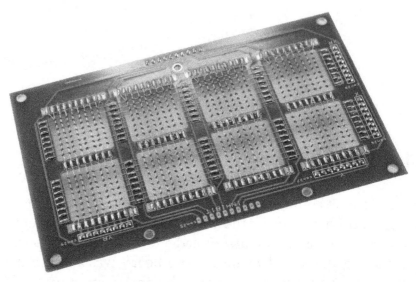

Figure 11-2 A Completed Core Assembly

Figure 11-3 Shows a completed (prototype) logic control and driver board.

Figure 11-3 Logic Control and Driver Board

The first step in testing is to check that all the ferrite cores are properly threaded onto the wires and that the wires are correctly soldered to the array board.

The power supply to drive the memory array must be able to deliver a current of approximately 1 Amp at 5 volts. Note that the peak current can be much higher than this. If for example a value of

00000000

Is being written to the memory core then all 8 inhibit drivers will be active along with 2 of the 16 core selection drivers and each will be carrying a current of 300mA. This gives a total peak current of 3.0A plus another 200mA for the control electronics which is a grand total of around 3.2 Amps. Luckily the read and write pulses are only 400nS in duration and so these peak currents are easily supplied by the power rail smoothing capacitors and the result is a much lower current draw from the power supply with the average current drawn at a refresh rate of 100KHz being approximately 350mA.

Once the logic control and core array boards have been fully assembled then they must be adjusted. Initially I used fixed value resistors throughout the design of this system but as testing progressed and it became clear that the system was functioning somewhat better than I had expected I decided to modify the design slightly so that it could potentially be used to drive existing magnetic core arrays. I will not be covering that in this book but it is worth considering some experimentation if you already have a magnetic core array which you want to try.

I will assume at this point that the two system boards have been correctly assembled and just need adjusting. If for any reason the system does not function as expected or draws excessive current then you should investigate that before proceeding.

All adjustment pots should be set to approximately mid point before starting the adjustment procedure.

Begin by fitting the two START jumpers in the external pulse positions (shorting the 2 right side pins on each jumper).

Apply short pulses of between 100 and 500nS to the START pin on the interface connector while using a scope to monitor pin 5 of U13. Adjust VR9 at the bottom right corner of the pcb for a pulse width on the scope of 400nS.

The top trace in figure 11-3 shows the correctly adjusted pulse.

This sets the timing of the sense amplifier sample pulse and may need slight adjustment later to properly match the board operation to your particular core array board.

The next step is to adjust the sense amplifier threshold setting for each sense amplifier. There are 8 preset pots for these adjustments and the bit numbers which each pot adjusts are in order from left to right starting with bit '0' at the left (VR1).

The setting is made by using a scope to observe the output of each sense amplifier while toggling the input to the amplifier between a '0' and a '1'.

This is most easily done by connecting a jumper wire to the appropriate input pin on the interface connector and alternately switching it between 0V and +5V.

The board should first be set to enable write mode (RW input high) and the memory enabled (_CE low).

A series of pulses must be applied to the START input as in the previous test step and the scope should be set to trigger on the rising edge of these pulses with the time base set to 200nS per division.

As the bit input is toggled between 0V and +5V then the output of the corresponding sense amplifier should be adjusted using the pot so that the falling edge of the output signal is approximately 250nS from the rising edge of the START pulse when a '0' is applied to the input and approximately 550nS from the rising edge of the START pulse when a '1' is applied to the input.

The bottom trace in figures 11-4 and 11-5 show how the pulses for a '0' input and '1' input should appear when the sense amplifier is correctly adjusted.

Notice that the second cursor line in these two images is set at the 400nS point from the rising edge of the trigger pulse.

This cursor line indicates the sample point for the sense input signal and so the aim is to provide the best signal differential around this point so that the system can determine if a '0' or a '1' is being read.

Improper setting of these adjustments will cause erratic operation of the memory system.

Note that until the adjustment is fairly close then the output of the sense amplifier may not switch at all and it may appear that the circuit is not working.

The operating range for the sense amplifier is very small and so requires proper adjustment before it will operate correctly.

If you wish to set a starting point for the adjustment then you can use a volt meter connected between 0V and the centre wiper of the pot you wish to adjust.

Begin by setting the pot so that the voltage at this point is 692mV.

Disconnect the meter before making further adjustments otherwise the sense amplifier will fail to operate correctly.

The output pins for each sense amplifier are identified in the table below.

Bit Number	Sense Amp Output
0	U15 pin 4
1	U15 pin 8
2	U15 pin 10
3	U22 pin 4
4	U22 Pin 8
5	U22 pin 10
6	U23 pin 4
7	U23 pin 10

Once all 8 sense amplifiers have been adjusted then the memory system should be fully functional and can be then be tested by connecting it to a host system.

The system presented in this book was intended to behave in a very similar fashion to an SRAM and the basic timing diagram for its operation is shown in figure 11-4.

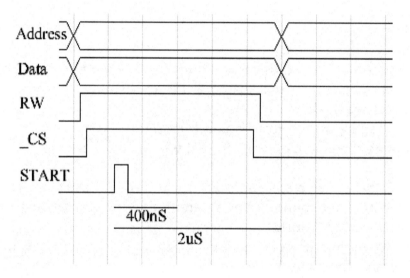

Figure 11-4 Memory Timing

Figure 11-2 shows the timing for a memory Write.

For a memory read the RW line is taken low and the data will be available on the data bus at the end of the 400nS period.

The entire memory cycle will be completed in 2uS.

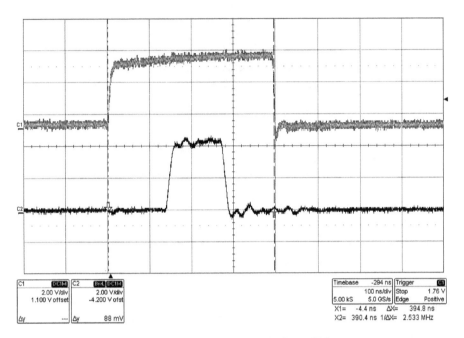

Figure 11-5 Sense Amp output for a '0' input

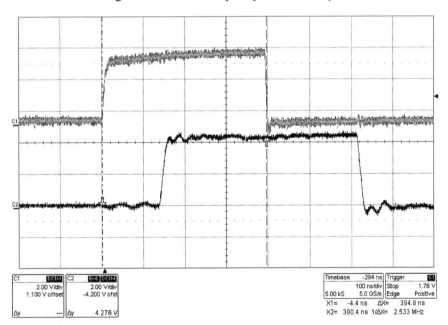

Figure 11-6 Sense Amp output for a '1' input

185

The exact method for testing you use will depend on what equipment you have access to but the basic specification of 400nS access time and memory cycle time of 2uS should be used as the absolute limit of operation. The maximum recommended read or write repetition rate is 250KHz.

The power supply used must be very stable and free from noise spikes otherwise erratic system operation may result.

If you wish to experiment with different cores then you may need to adjust the sense amplifiers for a different response and possibly adjust the sample pulse timer to a different setting.

The setting of 400nS I indicate in these descriptions was determined by both mathematical means and backed up by empirical tests and has proven to be suitable for the core types I specified earlier.

However these settings may not be suitable for alternative core types. The important point is to ensure that the pulse output from the sense amplifier can be differentiated between the '0' and '1' inputs and that at the sample point the correct value is latched into the read buffer.

Also you must consider that specific core types vary in response and there is a great deal of variability and interaction caused by the nature of the magnetic core array.

You therefore need to ensure a reasonable margin of acceptance in the design and as you can see in figures 11-3 and 11-4 the design I have presented has very good discrimination and so operates in a very stable manner even with variance in core behaviour or temperature.

If you have a scope with variable persistence and complex trigger then you can trigger on the START pulse and high RW control line while capturing the output from the sense amplifiers.

This will give a display which includes all the variations as the data value changes and each core response changes and goes a long way to explaining why I made such efforts to enhance the performance of the system.

The falling edge of the start pulse can then be adjusted using the sample timer adjustment pot to sample the sense amplifier output in the centre of the range as is shown in figure 11-6.

Figure 11-6 clearly shows how the signal outputs from the sense amplifiers varies due to the many interacting system characteristics and it also demonstrates how well the system is performing.

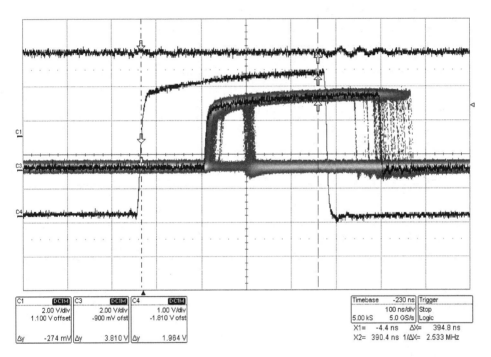

Figure 11-7 Sense Amplifier Signal Variation

The trace shown in figure 11-7 may seem to indicate that the signal output from the sense amplifier contains a great deal of noise but this is fully expected and why the sense amplifier needed careful design.

Transconductance

Another point worth making here relates to the seemingly simple arrangement for the sense amplifier and this possibly belies the amount of development work which I put into this part of the system design.

While the final circuit is very simple it makes use of some subtle design features which you may find interesting.

If you look at the sense amplifier circuit which I am repeating here in figure 11-5 you can see that the actual sense amplifier consists on nothing more than a single bipolar transistor.

This amplifier makes use of a feature of bipolar transistors called transconductance and the general configuration of this circuit is very important to its stable operation.

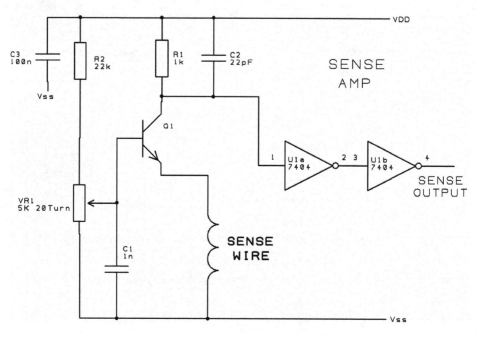

Figure 11-8 Sense Amplifier

Transconductance is the relationship between the current flowing in the output of the transistor, in this case its collector / emitter current and the voltage applied to the base of the transistor.

However there is an important element required in the reliable operation of a magnetic core memory system caused by a characteristic of the ferrite cores themselves.

The response and behaviour of the cores is somewhat temperature dependant and in fact most commercial magnetic core systems included either temperature compensation and had a temperature sensor located somewhere on the physical core.

Others even went to the trouble of installing the entire core assembly inside a temperature controlled oven and required a long heat up period before the memory could be used.

While I needed to make allowances for this core behaviour I still wanted to keep the circuits as simple as possible.

I therefore made use of a second characteristic of bipolar transistors which is that their performance is also temperature dependant.

By arranging the amplifier as a transconductance (voltage to current) amplifier and using a suitable collector resistor along with overall base reference current then the effective current gain changes caused by variations in transistor temperature could be used to automatically adjust the sense amplifier performance as the core temperature varied. The result is of course not providing as tightly controlled performance as could be achieved by using a temperature sensor and compensation circuits.

It does however provide very good characteristics for the sense amplifier without requiring additional components and complexity and during testing over a wide temperature range it has provided very consistent results.

If you decide to experiment with different resistor values for the sense amplifier then bear in mind that even if you set a particular base voltage to the correct threshold you must still ensure reliable response to variations in core temperature.

Once the memory system has been built and correctly adjusted I recommend connecting it to a host system and writing some simple code to fully test it.
Initially testing it using wire jumpers works very well but because of the nature of a magnetic core memory system there is a great deal of interaction between the various wires and drivers and so it is a good idea to test all possible signal permutations.

This requires that not only every possible data byte is written to and read from but also that every possible data value for each location is tried. In addition each data byte should be tested with values which are different from the other data byte values.
This results in tests where the minimum number of permutations is in excess of 4 million and so it is not practical to do this manually.

It is however very easy to carry out such testing using something like a microcontroller and this will also allow you to experiment with various ways to control the system.

The sorts of problems you are likely to encounter are entire data byte values cannot be stored at particular addresses.
In this case the most likely cause is a faulty X or Y wire driver circuit.
You may also find that certain bits in some addresses cannot be set.
This is generally caused by incorrect assembly of the core where some cores have been fitted with the wrong orientation.
You can determine which cores are at fault by setting specific addresses bearing in mind that the lower 3 bits of the address select the X driver and the upper 3 bits of the address select the Y driver.

If needed you can also unplug the array board and using a breadboard and wire jumpers you can connect a single core to the X, Y and sense / inhibit connections in order to test the ability of the system to read and write particular cores.

In general if you take a systematic and methodical approach to testing then you should end up with a fully functional magnetic core memory system.
It should however be stressed again that designing and building a functional magnetic core memory system which has arrays which consist of more than just a few cores is not an easy task.

You may need to experiment with the system configuration in order to get the results you need it you intend to connect the memory system to a host processor.
From that point you can start to experiment by designing your own host computer systems and this will really give you a vintage computer experience.

ℰℴ𝒳ℰ

Chapter 12 - Further Development

In the previous chapters we have assembled and tested a fully functional magnetic core memory system. In its current form it has a total of 64 bytes with each byte comprising 8 bits for a grand total of 512 bits.

This is of course tiny compared to the number of bits in even the smallest memory card which is available today. However I hope that this book has given you a feel for the efforts required by those involved in the original development of large scale memory technologies as how much was involved.

Our small memory system has taken some considerable effort to get working and that is with the benefit of progress made by previous development.

During the development of the system I have described it in this book I intentionally kept the design and explanations as uncomplicated as possible so that I could fully explain the important points at each step.

It should be noted however that if you wish to design your own system then you must ensure that each circuit is properly matched to the core array and that the timing and sequence for all control signals is correct for the response of the magnetic cores.

The driver circuits I described were designed to minimise the unwanted direct coupled impulse currents but if you want to improve the performance of the memory system then optimising the turn on and turn off times for these drivers may be more important.

This in turn may require careful consideration in the design of the sense amplifier to be sure that the wanted output signals can be separated from the selection wire impulse signals.

A further consideration in the system design is the total average current drawn by the combined wire driver and inhibit driver circuits. Careful design of these circuits can reduce the average current drawn by providing fast turn off times along with shorter on periods.

Further gains can be made by careful optimisation of the pulse sequence generator times although great care must be taken if changing the pulse timing as this has a major impact on all aspects of the system operation.

The relative timing of the various wire driver pulses is critical to the correct operation of the system and the drivers must switch in such a way that any overlap of driver currents is avoided. As with any inductive load there is an inherent delay in the start of a switching event and the actual response from the ferrite cores and this needs to be allowed for in the individual timing of the logic control signals.

You may be tempted to increase the number of cores in the array so that a greater memory capacity can be achieved but this will almost certainly require modification to most elements in the system.

I have carried out some testing based on the current performance of the system and it appears that the current design may support as many as 256 bytes which is of course 256 cores per mat.

This reduces the sense output signal level to around 15mV so adding more cores than this would almost certainly require a higher gain sense amplifier and gating of the sense wire signal to blank the direct coupled signal.

There are some simple but effective improvements that can be made although the interaction between the various system sections should always be considered.

For example the major limiting factor in the ability of the sense amplifier to discriminate between the X, Y select and inhibit wire direct coupled impulse currents and the wanted core switching currents is the amplitude of the impulse current spike.

A very easy way to improve the performance of the sense amplifier would be to produce a 'blanking' pulse at the start of the memory cycle which would prevent the direct coupled impulse currents from being detected by the sense amplifier. This would allow the effective gain of the sense amplifier to be increased and so improve the ability of the sense amplifier to detect the wanted signals while ignoring the unwanted signals.

In this case there is an inherent delay between application of the selection currents and the time taken for the magnetic core to switch magnetisation state. For the core used in the design presented in this book that time is approximately 200nS and so a blanking signal of around 200nS from the rising edge of the memory cycle start pulse would leave the sense amplifier free to concentrate on the wanted signal.

Many other such improvements could be included at the expense of added complication but as with most technologies they tended to get rapidly more complex as they developed.

The simple changes of improving selection pulse switching speeds and decreasing pulse generator times to match the increased switching rates reduced the overall memory cycle time from almost 3uS to approximately 1.2uS in this design and reduced memory access time from 800nS to just 400nS.

As with a standard SRAM or other memory types it would be possible to increase system RAM by simply adding additional memory devices and the same is true when using this system.

It would be very easy to increase RAM capacity by adding additional Magnetic core memory cards and providing suitable decoding to access them and in this way larger memory systems could be constructed while retaining the same basic design.

As I stated earlier the design I have presented here was never intended to be high performance or high capacity but I hope that I have demonstrated a system which is more than just a functional impersonation of a core memory.

This design represents a core memory system with a reasonable level of performance and an interface which has been made simple enough to allow implementation into experimental test systems.
It also uses standard parts and by avoiding the use of specialised parts such as coupling transformers and sense amplifier integrated circuits then it should be possible for anyone who is interested to build one of these units.
This should however be considered just a starting point and I hope that it will encourage further development and improvements.

Although 512 bytes may seem a very small amount of memory by modern standards it is worth considering that back when magnetic core memory was first being developed this amount of memory with this level of performance would have generated a great deal of interest and would have been worth a fortune.

ℒℋℰ

Chapter 13 - Assembling a Core Array

This book is not intended as an assembly guide and although I am making kits of parts available at the time of writing these may no longer be available as you read this.

However I thought that it may still be useful to some if I included a bit of information on how I went about assembling the memory array board in case you decide to build one.

As I have already mentioned in an earlier chapter the ferrite cores used in this design are fairly large compared to the tiny cores which were used in many commercial core memory systems. Even so they are still very small and each one measures just 1.2mm in diameter with a hole size of approximately 0.8mm which makes handling them very challenging. What makes this even more challenging is threading the cores correctly onto the very thin wires as each one must be orientated correctly if the memory system is to work as it should.

I purposefully designed the array board to be larger than it really needed to be in order to make the assembly process a bit easier but I still wanted to retain the appearance of a commercial magnetic core memory so the distance between each row and column of cores is just 2.5mm.

It may be possible for someone with very good eyesight to assemble a core array unaided but I highly recommend the use of a good optical stereo microscope. If you miss a single core or pass a wire through a core the wrong way it is very hard to correct.

A USB microscope tends to have a short delay between actions and the update of the image and this makes it unsuitable for such precision work. Also a non stereo microscope does not give the depth of field view which is required to ensure that the cores are properly threaded onto the wires.

Before starting assembly it is best to select a suitable type and size of enamelled copper wire as using the correct wire makes the whole process very much easier.

As I stated above the holes in the cores are 0.8mm and we need to thread 3 wires through each core and so it may seem that wires of up to 0.35mm can be used but unfortunately this is not the case.

If you look at the close up images of the assembled core as shown in Figure 13-1 then you can see that the cores are actually 45 degrees offset from the wire axis.

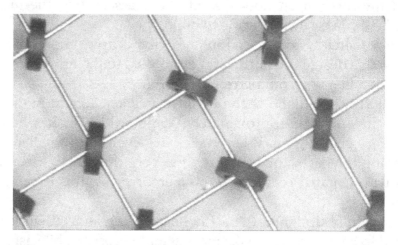

Figure 13-1 Close up of Array Cores

The cores have a thickness of around 0.25mm and this means that the effective hole size is very much smaller and a correspondingly smaller diameter wire must therefore be used. In fact I found that a wire of around 0.14mm was the easiest wire size to use. It is very thin but is still manageable if care is taken.

A second recommended feature of the selected wire is to use the so called 'solderable' enamelled wire as this avoids the need to scrape the insulation of the wire and with such thin wire it is very easy to accidentally cut through the wire. The main downside in using this type of wire is that it is harder to solder than clean copper wire and the iron also must be hotter than usual. I found that a temperature of 390C worked well but this does of course mean that you must be very careful not to overheat the solder pads on the circuit board otherwise they will lift off and the board will be ruined.
A bit of practice and soldering these wires becomes very easy. I recommend practising on a scrap board before starting assembly of the core.

There are a total of 512 cores to assemble on the board and it is important that the orientation of each is correct. I did try to keep this as simple as possible by laying out the board in such a way that each pair of array mats used an identical pattern although you should note that the pattern for the 'top' and 'bottom' row of mats is reversed.
The board is arranged so that the core magnetic field orientation is reversed for each Y column and in each mat as this makes threading the Sense and Inhibit wire much easier. It does however mean that careful attention must be paid to assembling the cores onto the selection wires.

Note that each column of cores is reversed and each top and bottom mat is also reversed but all top and bottom pairs are identical.
It is very important that each core is correctly orientated within the core assembly otherwise the system will fail to operate correctly.

See figure 13-2 to see the correct core orientation.

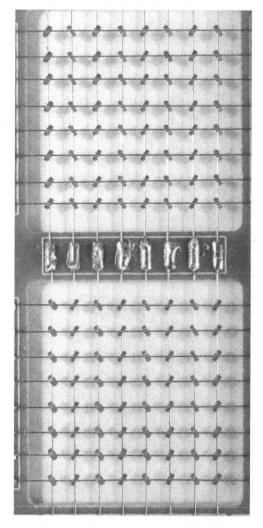

Figure 13-2 Ferrite Core Orientation

Once you have the required parts and tools prepared then the method of assembly I found easiest was as follows:

Fitting the X Selection Wires

1) Start by Soldering the left end of the top X wire to the board.
2) Cut the wire so that it is at least 200mm longer than the board.
3) Thread 32 cores onto the free end of the wire and then raise the wire so that they all slide down to the end which is soldered to the board. Figure 13-3 shows how this looks.
4) Lay the wire flat and loosely secure the free end so that it is roughly straight and in line with the appropriate pads on the board.
5) Slide the cores so that each cut out in the board has 8 cores in it.
6) Gently pull the wire so that it is straight and in line with the proper pads and then solder each joint from left to right. Re-tension wire after you solder each joint as it will have a tendency to slacken. Be sure that each cut out has 8 cores before soldering the wire.
7) Once the last joint at the right side of the board has been soldered then trim the wire to length.
8) Repeat this for all 16 X wires.

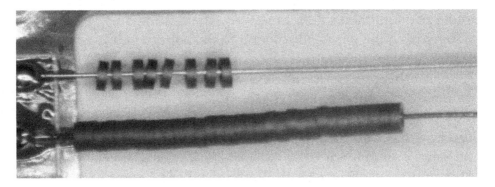

Figure 13-3 Sliding the cores onto the wires

At this point all 512 cores are threaded onto the X wires and each board cut out has 64 cores in it with 8 cores on each X wire.

The next step takes a bit of practice but is not too difficult once you get the feel for it.

Fitting the Y Selection Wires

1) Cut a 200mm length of wire and carefully straighten one end of it for approximately 80mm.
2) Very carefully use the tweezers to select and position each core, starting at the bottom X wire and slide the Y wire carefully through the core. Be sure as the wire passes through each core that the core is correctly orientated. Note that the cores in the top row of mats are reversed compared to the cores in the bottom row of mats.
Be careful not to push the wire too firmly as it will just kink and you will then have to pull it back out and start again.
Also be sure not to leave any cores on the left side of the wire.
3) once the wire has been passed through all 16 cores in the column then solder the top end to the appropriate solder pad.
4) Gently pull the wire to tension it and align it with the centre solder pad and then solder the wire to the centre pad.
5) Re-tension the wire and solder it to the bottom pad.
6) trim the wire to length.
7) Repeat this process for all 32 Y wires being careful to observe the correct core orientation.

You now have all X and Y wires in place and the last step is to fit the Sense / Inhibit wires.
Although these wires pass through a total of 64 cores each they are fairly easy to fit as the cores are now fairly stable.

1) Cut a length of wire approximately 500mm long.
2) Thread the wire though all 8 cores in the left column of the first mat.

3) Pull the wire almost all the way through and solder the end to the pad. Gently pull the wire to straighten it.

4) Loop the wire back on itself and thread back down through each core in the same mat but in the next Y column. Leave a small loop as shown.

5) Continue threading the wire up and down through the 8 cores in each mat X row until all 8 Y columns in the mat have been completed.

6) Solder the end of the wire to the pad and then trim the wire to length.

7) Repeat this process for all 8 mats.

The core array is now complete although I recommend fitting some clear protective covers to prevent damaging the fragile array.

Figure 13-4 shows an almost completed array board.

Figure 13-4 Almost Complete Array Board

Assembling the core may at first seem almost impossible but after a little practice it becomes surprisingly easy and does not take as long as it first seems that it will.

I was eventually able to assemble a core board in just 4 hours but the first attempt took much longer.

It is certain that there is a real feeling of achievement when the core is assembled and even more so when it works.

They are also very interesting to look at and the design of this core is no unlike a core designed and manufactured back in the 1960's and as such it represents a historically important piece of computer technology.

Chapter 14 - Rope Memory

While I do not intend to go into much detail about the so called 'Rope Memory' I felt that no discussion about magnetic core memory would be complete without at least mentioning it.

The memory system we developed in this book is a type of memory referred to as Random Access Memory or RAM and it is used as general purpose memory by the host system. In general each memory location in RAM can be read from and written to or modified randomly by the system in which it resides. Hence the term random access.

This implies that each bit within this memory space must be modifiable individually and so each bit must be completely separate and be able to store whatever value is written to it.

For that reason each individual ferrite core in a random access memory system will only be able to store a single bit of information. You will no doubt have noticed in our system development that we went to a great deal of trouble to properly decode each individual bit in each individual byte so that we could store whatever values we wanted. We could then modify these values in a random way so we had developed a true random access memory system.

Anyone even remotely familiar with computer systems will know that there is a second major class of memory which is referred to as 'Read Only Memory' or ROM. As its name implies it is a type of memory which stores data in such a way that it can only be read from and not written to.

The corresponding version of this type of memory which uses ferrite cores as the data storage medium is known as 'Rope Memory' for reasons which will become apparent shortly.

Actually in rope memory the data bits are modified so are technically not really read only although the data value that is returned by a rope memory system is always the same for each memory location. It is therefore suitable as a read only data storage solution and in fact is one of the most robust and reliable types of ROM which has so far been devised.

As I said I will not be going into too much detail and although I will be developing a rope memory system in the near future that is for another book.

I will however cover the basics of this fascinating variation on the ferrite core memory technology as it is as ingenious as the random access type which we have already looked at.

How is Data Read from Rope Memory

In this book we have investigated in some detail how ferrite cores are used to store data by controlling their magnetisation state and the particular magnetisation state of each individual core represented a single data bit. We were able to retrieve the stored data from the ferrite cores by applying carefully controlled current pulses and detecting the output pulses generated in sense wires running through the cores.

In our system a core which changed state during a read cycle were deemed to be storing a bit value of '1' and cores which did not change state were storing a '0'.

Rope memory works in a very similar way in that ferrite cores are again used to represent bit values which we can read by passing currents through wires running through the cores and detecting the pulses created by any cores which change magnetisation state.

There is however a fundamental difference in the way in which rope memory is constructed which makes the data values consistent and cause the memory to always return the same data values.

This type of memory also makes incredibly efficient use of the ferrite cores by storing more than a single data bit in each individual core. If you are not familiar with this concept then it may sound very odd that a single core can store more than one piece of information but hopefully I can explain the way in which it does this.

Figure 14-1 shows a single core with a single selection pulse wire and a single sense wire running through it and this arrangement allows us to store a single bit of information. If we erase the core and then read the core back by applying first a pulse in one direction for the erase phase and then a pulse in the opposite direction for the read phase then we will always detect a '1' in the sense wire.

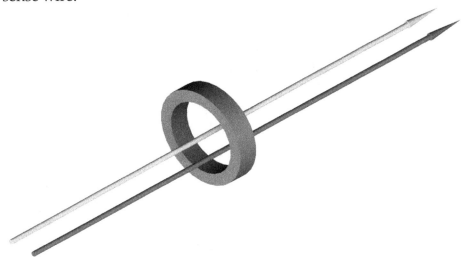

Figure 14-1 Rope Memory - Single Sense Wire

This may not sound very useful as we are always going to read back the same '1' value but as that is exactly what we want for this bit then that is fine.

Let us assume that for 4 bits of data we want a binary value of :

0011

Then we can now assume we have successfully stored the first bit which gives us:

xxx1

The obvious question is of course how do we go about storing the remaining bit values and the answer is not only simple but also very elegant. Figure 14-2 shows how we can do this.

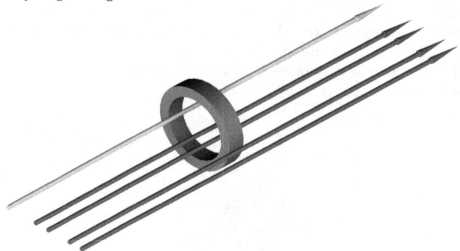

Figure 14-2 Rope Memory - 4 Sense Wires

In this diagram I have added 3 additional sense wires to the core although we still have a single selection pulse wire running through the core (green). In fact only 2 of the sense wires pass through the core and the other 2 bypass it.

If we now erase and then read the core in this configuration then the sense wires will return a data value of:

0011

And so not only have we successfully stored the required 8 bit data value but we have done this using a single core and it is also read only in as much as an erase and read cycle will always return the same data value.

In fact we can store far more bits in a single core by simply adding more sense wires and threading them so that the wires pass through the core when a '1' is required and they bypass the core when a '0' is wanted.

An added advantage in this method is that we can create systems which use any date bit width and you may be aware that many older systems had odd word sizes which were not restricted to multiples of 2, 4 or 8.

Some though on this and we can see that we are not limited to storing individual data byte values in a single core but if we want to we can store multiple bytes of information in each core as long as we know how to address the individual bytes within a block of data.

Rope memory systems could easily have well over 200 sense wires running through each core and so could store 25 or more data bytes in a single core. This made them extremely efficient and compact along with being almost totally immune to data loss should power be lost while they were in operation.

Once assembled it could also be potted to protect the wires and cores and this made them almost indestructible.

The next question is of course how we go about reading data from individual cores and this is achieved in a very similar way to the method we used in the system we developed in this book.

Inhibit Wires in a Rope Memory

Figure 14-3 shows how we can selectively read data from one of 3 cores.

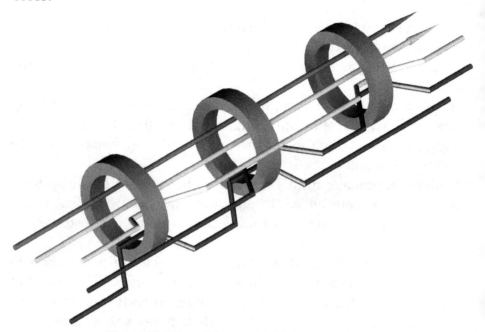

Figure 14-3 Rope Memory Multiple Inhibit Wires

In this diagram I have included just one sense wire (Red) to keep the diagram clear but many more sense wires could be added if required to store more data.

The green wire is the Set / Reset selection wire and the blue and grey wires are the 3 inhibit wires.

During operation the Set / Reset wire is used to attempt to clear and read the cores but it is the combination of the Set / Reset wires and the inhibit wires which determine which core is selected. It is effectively the reverse of the way in which cores are selected in the memory system which we developed.

To select a specific core then two of the inhibit wires along with the Set / Reset wire must be energised and if you look at figure 14-3 then the two inhibit wires which are energised are the two blue wires. The grey wire is not carrying any current so this means that the only core which has two current carrying inhibit wires passing through it is the centre core.

This means that the data appearing on the sense wires is the data 'stored' in the centre core and as long as this core is selected the returned data value will always be the same.

We can select any of the cores in this manner by simply applying the correct pattern of currents to the Set / Reset and inhibit wires and this allows us to selectively read the data stored in any of the cores.

That is all there is to rope memory and once the methods for using ferrite cores to store data is understood then understanding rope memory is simple.

As a final part of this explanation I said that memory of this type was called rope memory for a particular reason so I have included an image of a rope memory assembly in figure 14-4 which will hopefully explain the name.

Figure 14-4 Rope Memory Close up

This type of rope memory was in very wide spread use for many years and it was used in many thousands of applications from relatively simple electronic calculators to getting man to the moon and back.

For anyone interested in this type of technology it can provide an almost unlimited source of further projects or investigation and experimentation.

If so far you have only worked with digital devices such as modern microcontrollers then it can be hard to imagine just how much can be achieved with magnetic core systems.

For example it would be theoretically possible to store the entire text of this book in a single core if enough sense wires could be woven through and around it although the number of sense amplifiers may make this impractical. It does however open up a whole new way of looking at digital systems that otherwise may not be considered.

The rope memory assembly shown in figure 14-4 is from another project I am currently working on and uses 192 data wires to give a total of 24 bytes of 8 bit data stored in each core.

The three cores shown in the image could actually store the following block of text.

ABCDEFGHIJKLMNOPQRSTUVWXYZabcdefghijklmnopqrstuvw xyz0123456789HelloWorld

That is 576 bits using just 3 cores which is an incredibly efficient and reliable way to store data. Once the rope memory has been assembled then only physical damage will cause the cores to return the incorrect bit values

Well I hope that you found this book interesting and that it has prompted you to look further into magnetic core memory systems.

Appendix A – Magnetic Core Memory Summary

The following table gives a summary of the magnetic core memory system.

Memory Capacity Bytes	64
Memory Capacity Bits	512
Access time	400nS
Cycle time - Read	1.9uS
Cycle time - Write	1.9uS
Mats	8
Selection Wires	16
Wire Currents	320mA
Power Supply	+5V
Average current consumption	550mA @ 150,000 cycles per second
Transistors used	120
IC's used	31
Ferrite Core dimensions (mm)	1.2 x 0.2 x 0.8

List of Figures

Figure 1-1 An Abacus - some dating back over 4000 years 7
Figure 1-2 Early mechanical calculator 9
Figure 1-4 Rope magnetic core memory (ROM) 16
Figure 1-5 A single memory plane 17
Figure 1-6 Close up view of a typical memory core 18
Figure 1-7 Comparison of Core Dimensions 21
Figure 1-8 Close up View of 1.2mm Ferrite Core 22
Figure 2-1 'Normal' ferrite material response 27
Figure 2-2 Magnetic Filed Below Critical Threshold 29
Figure 2-3 Current at Threshold 30
Figure 2-4 Applied Current Higher than Critical Threshold 31
Figure 2-5 Single memory core array 35
Figure 2-6 Assembled Memory Array Board 36
Figure 2-7 Partially Assembled Memory Array Board 39
Figure 2-8 Read Current Polarities 40
Figure 2-9 Write Current Polarities 41
Figure 3-1 Un-polarised Magnetic core 46
Figure 3-2 Flipping the Magnetisation 47
Figure 3-3 Magnetisation hysteresis 48
Figure 3-4 Flipping the magnetisation again 49
Figure 3-5 Magnetisation hysterisis again 50
Figure 3-6 Completing the Magnetisation loop 50
Figure 3-7 Ferrite flip output 52
Figure 3-8 Ferrite Core Test Rig 53
Figure 3-9 Fast Rising edge coupling response 55
Figure 3-10 Fast Falling edge coupling response 56
Figure 3-11 Magnetisation switch pulse output 57
Figure 3-12 Coupling output with slow rising edge 58
Figure 3-13 Coupling output with slow falling edge 58
Figure 3-14 Magnetisation switch with slow rising current 60
Figure 3-15 Magnetisation switch with slow falling current 60
Figure 4-1 Ferrite Core size Comparison 70
Figure 4-2 Ferrite Cores Orientation 71
Figure 4-3 Core X selection wires 72
Figure 4-4 Core Y selection wires 73
Figure 4-5 Sense wire added 74
Figure 4-6 Inhibit Wire Added 75
Figure 4-7 Sense and Inhibit wire detail 76
Figure 4-8 Stacked Core Array 78
Figure 4-9 Simple Single Layer Core 79

Figure 4-10 Single Layer Mat Perspective View 79
Figure 4-11 Close up of Part of Array Mat 80
Figure 4-12 Magnetic Core Array Board 81
Figure 5-1 Single Mat X and Y selection decoder Concept 88
Figure 5-2 Array X and Y selection decoder Concept 89
Figure 5-3 Inhibit Control Concept 89
Figure 5-4 Core Arrangement Simplified concept 90
Figure 5-5 Conceptual Memory System Data Flow 93
Figure 5-6 Adding Control Logic 95
Figure 6-1 Memory Cycle Start Circuit 99
Figure 7-1 Magnetisation switch Output Signal 104
Figure 7-2 Sense Amplifier Circuit 106
Figure 7-3 Sense Output with no Magnetisation Switch 108
Figure 7-4 Sense Output with Magnetisation Switch 109
Figure 7-5 Sense Output with Negative Magnetisation Switch 110
Figure 7-6 Sense Amp with Trigger and Latch 112
Figure 7-7 Sense Latch Control Signals 113
Figure 7-8 Sense Latch Output 114
Figure 7-9 Coupled Output with faster Rising Edge 116
Figure 7-10 Output Signals with Faster Rising Edge 117
Figure 8-1 Wire Driver Circuit 123
Figure 8-2 Wire Driver Bridge Circuit 125
Figure 8-3 Wire Read/Write Selection Circuit 130
Figure 8-4 Selection Wire Strobe Control Circuit 134
Figure 9-1 Inhibit Driver Circuit 144
Figure 9-2 Sense Amplifier Circuit 146
Figure 9-3 Combined Sense Amp and Inhibit Driver 146
Figure 9-4 Inhibit Strobe Decoder 149
Figure 10-1 Memory System Structure 156
Figure 10-2 Memory Cycle Start Circuit 158
Figure 10-3 Address Decoder 160
Figure 10-4 Timing Pulse Generator 165
Figure 10-5 X and Y Driver Control Logic 166
Figure 10-6 Wire Drivers and Control Logic 167
Figure 10-7 Phase Control Logic 169
Figure 10-8 Inhibit Strobe Control Circuit 171
Figure 10-9 Inhibit Control and Driver Circuit 172
Figure 10-10 Data Flow in Read Phase One 175
Figure 10-11 Read Phase Data Restore 175
Figure 10-12 First Phase of Write Cycle - Erase 176
Figure 10-13 Phase Two of Write Cycle 176
Figure 11-1 A Single Completed Core Mat 179
Figure 11-2 A Completed Core Assembly 180
Figure 11-3 Logic Control and Driver Board 180
Figure 11-4 Memory Timing 184
Figure 11-5 Sense Amp output for a '0' input 185
Figure 11-6 Sense Amp output for a '1' input 185
Figure 11-7 Sense Amplifier Signal Variation 187

List of Figures

Figure 11-8 Sense Amplifier...188
Figure 13-1 Close up of Array Cores..198
Figure 13-2 Ferrite Core Orientation 200
Figure 13-3 Sliding the cores onto the wires 201
Figure 13-4 Almost Complete Array Board 203
Figure 14-1 Rope Memory - Single Sense Wire...207
Figure 14-2 Rope Memory - 4 Sense Wires 208
Figure 14-3 Rope Memory Multiple Inhibit Wires..210
Figure 14-4 Rope Memory Close up...211

·